高职高专英语教学改革新教材

Public Practical English
公共实用英语学习指导

顾　问　杨广俊

主　编　李　红

副主编　刘俊花　张艳丽

编　委　李　红　刘俊花　张艳丽　李　磊
　　　　陈　航　杨　静　李振俭　王志江

上海交通大学出版社

内 容 提 要

　　《公共实用英语》是按照《高职高专教育英语课程教学基本要求》和《全国成人高等教育英语课程教学基本要求(非英语专业专科用)》而编写的,同时还参考了"高等学校英语应用能力考试大纲"和"大学英语四级考试大纲"。

　　本书为《公共实用英语》教材(第一册,第二册)的配套学习指导书。内容包括教材中所有练习的答案、听力材料、翻译参考译文、写作范文等。

图书在版编目（C I P）数据

公共实用英语学习指导/李红主编.—上海：上海交通大学出版社，2007
　　ISBN978-7-313-04627-7

　　Ⅰ.公… Ⅱ.李… Ⅲ.英语—高等学校：技术学校—教学参考资料 Ⅳ.H31

中国版本图书馆CIP数据核字（2006）第144541号

公共实用英语学习指导
李 红 主编
上海交通大学出版社出版发行
（上海市番禺路877号 邮政编码200030）
电话：64071208 出版人：韩建民
上海崇明南海印刷厂 印刷 全国新华书店经销
开本：787mm×960mm 1/16 印张：14.5 字数：267千字
2007年1月第1版 2007年1月第1次印刷
印数：1—4050
ISBN978-7-313-04627-7/H·632 定价：22.00元

前　　言

　　《公共实用英语》是按照《高职高专教育英语课程教学基本要求》和《全国成人高等教育英语课程教学基本要求（非英语专业专科用）》而编写的，同时还参考了"高等学校英语应用能力考试大纲"和"大学英语四级考试大纲"。本教材是为提高日校及成人教育学生英语水平，推进高职高专英语教学改革而编写的英语知识综合实用教材。编写本套教材的过程是一种探索编撰集学习与参与考试为一体的英语教材的有益尝试。

　　本套教材遵循语言应用发展和非母语学习的一般规律，注意高职高专的职业语言应用的需要，关心兴趣对语言学习的促进作用，使教材兼生活性、趣味性、科学性于一体。作者根据教学的实践经验，依据知识要点，结合学生特点和社会职业应用要求，吸取其他教材的长处，进行了系统的研究、探索和创新。

　　本套教材分为教材（两册）和学习指导。每册教材各十个单元，每单元包括谚语（Proverbs）、听力训练（Listening Practice）、口语训练（Oral Practice）、阅读训练（Reading Practice：Text A ，Text B）、写作训练（Writing Practice）、拓宽训练（Further Practice），并附有生词表和短语表。

　　本套教材的特点是：新颖、精美、实用、易学、面广。所选内容贴近生活、题材广泛、难易适中、文章精炼优美、思想健康向上。以应用为目的，"学、练"结合，"听、说、读、写、译"协调并进，加强英语综合应用能力的培养，注重语言学习和实际应用的结合，涉猎了身边的日常生活、社会变化、科技进步、国际政治和经济，尽量扩大实际应用频度较高的词汇，培养学生的英语交际和基本的英语公文应用能力。教材按照体系需要，在健康的主体价值原则指导下，使语言内容材料的菁华兼容并蓄，增强了知识性、趣味性，在学生学习英语的同时，让学生接受正确的人生价值观的熏陶，增加社会阅历知识。本套教材还关注高职高专和成人专科教育的层次和学生的具体情况，提供了大量的材料，教师可根据教学中的实际情况有选择地进行讲解，既不让学生重复低层次循环，也不超越学生层次要求，增强学生语言学习的信心。相信通过本套教材的学习，将会使学生在愉快中完成预设的教学目标。

　　本套教材还注意了教材与学习指导书的整体学习效能的相互促进作用。为巩固英语学习效果，提高英语交际水平和英语应试能力，除了教科书和学习指导书之外，我们还编写了《大学英语应试综合指南》。《公共实用英语》提供了经典的和现代典型的英语材料，吸收了典型的英语考试题型，是一套体系完整、内容系统的高职高专层次教材;《公共实用英语学习指导》是与教材相配套的、具有针对性的辅助教材;《大学英语应试综合指南》是在《公共实用英语》及学习指导书的基础上,融学习资料、检验学习效果和应用能力的教学书籍,是此阶段学生参加各类等级考试的有效指导书。

教材的编写得到了本书顾问——河南省高等院校外语教学委员会主任委员、郑州大学杨广俊教授的精心指导,提出了宝贵的建议。主要编写人员是多年来一直从事高职高专英语教学的一线教师,有切实的体验和丰富的实际教学经验。主编李红同志主持了本套教材的构思、组织、编写及全书的统稿工作;副主编刘俊花、张艳丽同志协助主编做了统稿以及文字的初审工作;参加编写的还有李磊、陈航、杨静、李振俭、王志江同志。

本套教材的编写得到了方舒燕、陈犁等同志的大力支持,郭卫同志对全书进行了审阅,在此表示感谢;我们兼采百家之言,吸取了有益的学术精华,对本套教材所参考到的资料的作者深表感谢;对编写过程中王铮同志协助所作的部分文字工作表示感谢。虽然编著者博采众长,追求精益求精,但是,书中难免出现不足之处,欢迎读者和专家指正。

编　者

2006 年 8 月

Contents

Public Practical English
(Book One)

Public Practical English
(Book Two)

Public Practical English

（Book One）

Public Practical English

(Book One)

Unit 1 A New Beginning

Key & Difficult Points：(重点、难点)

New Words

introduce, pleasure, professor, smooth, melt, mess, shoot, hang, suggest, major, adjustment, disappointment, competitive, intend, reward, relax, value, available, process, subject, construction, calculation, requirement, broaden, purpose, advice

Phrases & Expressions

by the way, make friends, wait for, have a good time, a great deal of, stress on, as a result, prepare for, make sure, in fact, key to, be out, be fair to, go it alone, have to do, it is … that … 强调句句型, find + *n. / pron.* + 宾语不足语, make 为使意动词后跟复合宾语的情况

Exercises

Listening Practice：Section B (Exercise 1, Exercise 2)

Reading Practice： **Text A**　Part 2　Words & Structure (Exercise 1, 2)

　　　　　　　　　　Part 3　Translation (Exercise 2)

　　　　　　　　Text B　Part 2　Words & Structure (Exercise 2)

　　　　　　　　　　Part 3　Translation (Exercise 1)

Writing Practice

Further Practice：Part 1　Multiple Choice

Listening Practice

Key to

Exercise

Directions: *In this section, you will hear a dialogue. At the end of the dialogue, there are some questions. Listen carefully and answer the questions.*

1. Chatting online
2. a good way
3. confused
4. bye for now
5. None of your business
6. CWYL, LTNS

Tape-script

Talk about Abbreviations Used Online

Li Hong: What are you doing tonight?

Mike: Chatting online.

Li Hong: Again?

Mike: Mm. I really enjoy chatting with friends online. It's such a good way to communicate with each other.

Li Hong: Yes, but I am confused when I come across some abbreviations. I don't know what they all mean.

Mike: I can tell you some. If someone writes "Fever", it means "forever", "BFN" means "bye for now", "BS" means "big smile", and so on.

Li Hong: Oh, I see. How interesting! Now I can guess what these abbreviations might mean.

Mike: I know quite a lot of these abbreviations. If you like, I can tell you more.

Li Hong: Yes, I will be grateful if you can tell me more.

4

Mike:	"CWYL" means "chat with you later", "LTNS" means "long time no see", "IYSS" means "if you say so", "NOYB" means "None of your business."
Li Hong:	Oh, really. I remember I ran once into "TTYL" while chatting with somebody online. Let me have a guess. Does it mean "talk to you later"?
Mike:	That's right. You are really smart.

Section B

Key to

Exercise 1

Directions: *Listen to a passage and decide whether the following statements are true or false. Write "T" for True and "F" for False.*

1~5　F　T　F　F　T

Exercise 2

Directions: *Listen to the passage again and choose the best answer.*

1~5　D　C　C　A　C

Tape-script

How Did John Survive in Italy?

My cousin, John, is a university student. Last year he went to Italy and stayed there for two months. I was surprised that John was able to have such a long holiday because he never has any money.

"How did you manage it, John?" I asked. "I thought you were going to stay for two weeks."

"It was easy," John answered. "I got a job."

"A job!" I exclaimed. "What did you do?"

"I gave English lessons to a grocer," John answered. "His name is Luigi. We have become great friends."

"But you're not a teacher," I said.

"I told Luigi I couldn't teach," John explained. "But he insisted on having conversation lessons. He wanted to practice his English. He has a lot of American customers, so it is important for him to speak English. I spent three hours a day talking to him. In return he gave me a room, three meals a day and a little pocket money."

"Did your pupil learn much English?" I asked.

"I don't know," John said, "but I learned a lot of Italian!"

Oral Practice

参考译文

对话1

情景

李涛和莎莉是好朋友,他们是大二的学生。晚饭后,他俩在校园散步。郭华是一年级的新生,刚来的第一天李涛热情地接待了他,因此李涛和郭华熟悉。现在他们碰巧相遇。

李涛： 喂,鲍勃。再一次见到你很高兴。你好吗?

郭华： 我很好,谢谢。你呢,李先生?

李涛： 不错。我想要介绍你给我的朋友莎莉史密斯认识。莎莉来自美国,她正在我们这学习中药。

郭华： 很高兴遇见你,莎莉史密斯小姐。

莎莉： 遇见你也很高兴。哦,请叫我莎莉吧。

李涛： 顺便问一下,鲍勃,这个星期五晚上学生会将举行一个宴会。你愿意来吗?

郭华： 为什么不? 咱们一块去那里共同度过美好时光。我确信这也是一个我们交新朋友的好机会。

对话 2

情景

布朗先生是北京大学新来的客座教授,他从未到过此地。因此,张先生去机场接他。下面是他们的谈话:

张: 请问,您是来自美国的布朗教授吗?

布朗: 是的。我是汤姆斯布朗。

张: 您好,我是来自北京大学的张立华。

布朗: 您好,先生……?

张: 哦,张。我姓张。立华是我的名。

布朗: 遇见你很高兴,张先生。

张: 遇见你我也很高兴,布朗教授。飞行途中好吗?

布朗: 非常好。相当顺利。

张: 听到这些很高兴。我能帮你拿手提箱吗?

布朗: 好的,谢谢你。你提那个小点的好吗?

张: 可以。教授,现在我们走吧?

布朗: 好,我们走。

张: 请这边走。我们的车等在那里。

布朗: 好。

Reading Practice

Text A

参考译文

大学——新的开端

帕特森非常了解新生:了解他们的希望、梦想和顾虑。她在迎新致辞的开场白中说:

"它使我想起了积雪消融的早春时节。你无论踩到哪里都会溅起水花。即便是又冷又湿,我不能怨恨那些日子,因为它们预示着春天的来临。新生的到来使学校一团糟,但我也同样不讨厌这件事。新生来到镇上,就像绿色的幼苗从四处冒出来,寻找阳光。当他们的脸从宿舍的窗户里探出来时,就好像古老的大树上绽出的新芽。也许有人会担心阳光是否充足,土壤是否肥沃,霜冻是否降临,可是对幼苗和大学新生来说,能够存活,能够跨进大学的校门,就足够了。

"是的,今天是新生活的开始。昨天你们还是妈妈的孩子,住在家里。今天,你们已经是大学的新生,开始独立生活了。'新生!'我喜欢这个称呼。这个称呼本身让人想到一个问题。我们在读这个词时,应该把重音放在'新'上呢,还是放在'生'上?怎么读都可以。无论你把成年看作是人生的旅程还是终点,今天无疑是你们人生道路上的一大步。新生的欢喜和新生的忧愁都挂在我周围每一张年轻的脸上。"

"大学是令人激奋的时期,也许还是你一生中最开心的时光。但同时也是进行不少重大调整和经历一些挫败的时期。如今,大多数研究领域的竞争都已经非常激烈了。你们必须努力学习,作好充分准备,才能进入这些领域。信息爆炸对需求信息的人提出了更高的要求。因此,对大学生活来说,越来越需要有一个安排更合理的开端。现在,学校里针对新生的课程越来越受欢迎,作为新同学,你们应该选修一些这样的课程,它们能帮助你为将来学习难度更大的课程作准备。你们应该确保自己学会很好地阅读、写作和发言,不要惧怕那些迫使你思考的课程。思考可以令人兴奋并且大有裨益。同时,花一些时间享受生活——放松一下,注意营养,笑口常开。让大学生活如你所愿,成为美妙而有价值的经历。祝大家好运!"

Exercises

Part 1   Reading Comprehension

1. Directions：*Choose the best answer according to the text.*

1)~5)   D C A C B

2. Directions：*Answer the following questions according to the text.*

1) College is an exciting time.

2) It's her favorite day.

3) He is beginning a new life.

Part 2   Words and Structure

1. Directions：*Match an expression in **Column B** which is similar in meaning to the **ONE** in **Column A**.*

1)～5) j d c b a   6)～10) i h g f e

2. Directions: *Fill in each of the blanks with an appropriate word or phrase from the box. Change the form if necessary.*

1) abbreviated   2) please
3) majority   4) professional
5) make sure   6) as a result

Part 3　Translation

1. Directions: *Translate the following passage into Chinese.*

美国的大学和学院在考虑留学生入学资格时要看一些东西。首先,学校要查看学生在中学、先前的学院或大学的成绩。其次,学校要考虑学生的英文能力。大多数学校需要学生参加英语测试如托福考试。许多国家定期进行这种测试。最后,学校看学生的经济情况。在美留学生学习的时候不能工作。因此学生必须向学校表明他们有足够的钱来支付学费和生活费。

2. Directions: *Translate the following sentences into English.*

1) She exclaimed in delight when she saw the presents.
2) Her expression suggested anger.
3) You always get value for money at that shop.
4) It will be difficult for you to smooth over your differences after so many years.
5) This kitchen is a mess.

Text B

参考译文

忠　告
基思·戴弗林

我最强烈的忠告是要珍惜你所受教育的广度。在今天或明天的世界上取得成功的关键是一种学习的能力。

在中学里你有老师。但当你在以后工作时,你可能就要自个儿干了。大学则是两者之间的一个过渡场所。教授在那儿帮助你、指引你。但是作为教师,他们试图"教"你的最重要的东西是如何学习。例如,你的数学教授并不是在那儿教你数学。他/她在那儿是通过示范告诉你如何学习数学,并在这一过程中帮助你。这跟中学大不一样。

我的第二点忠告是对那些你不喜欢或你认为永远也学不好的科目要下最大的苦功。对很多学生来说,他们不喜欢的科目是数学。但对很多职业道路来说,数学都是他们取得成功所需要掌握的。对建筑工人和工程师来说,几何是你应该掌握的。对未来的教师来说,为了判断你的测试对学生是否公平,你需要统计学。即使对某个只想待在家里做妈妈的人来说,持家也需要进行计算。事实上,我说的这番话在你们面对任何一门科目时对你们大家都适用。大学之所以规定所有那些毕业要求并不是为了让你们受苦。它们是为了帮助你开阔视野,并使你们准备好最充分地度过一生。

我的最后一点忠告是享受你们的大学生活。我常听人们说,大学不是真实世界,在大学读几年书的目的是为了未来"在真实世界"的生活作好准备。这话不对。在以后几年中你不会停止生活。你在大学的时间并不是为以后作的准备生活。它是你生活中的几年。它就是"真实世界"。因此就享受你作为一名学生的时间,充分地过你的新的"真实生活"吧。

Exercises

Part 1　Reading Comprehension

1. Directions: *Choose the best answer according to the text.*

1)~5)　A　B　B　D　D

2. Directions: *Answer the following questions according to the text.*

1) Most of the jobs will be new to the students.

2) 2.

3) Because college life is also part of students' lives.

4) Open.

Part 2　Words and Structure

1. Directions: *Match an expression in **Column B** which is similar in meaning to the **ONE** in **Column A**.*

1)~5)　i d g c j　　　　6)~10)　e h b f a

2. Directions: *Fill in each of the blanks with an appropriate word from the box.*
 Change the form if necessary.

1) calculation　　　　　　2) statistical

3) probability　　　　　　4) requires

5) guidance　　　　　　　6) construct

Part 3　Translation

1. Directions: *Translate the following passage into Chinese.*

1) 在中学里你有老师。但当你在以后工作时，你可能就要自个儿干了。大学则是两者之间的一个过渡场所。教授在那儿帮助你、指引你。但是作为教师，他们试图"教"你的最重要的东西是如何学习。

2) 我常听人们说，大学不是真实世界，在大学读几年书的目的是为了未来"在真实世界"的生活作好准备。这话不对。在以后几年中你不会停止生活。你在大学的时间并不是为以后作的生活准备。它是你生活中的几年。它就是"真实世界"。

2. Directions: *Translate the following sentences into English.*

1) The gangsters ran into the bar and started shooting it up.

2) She majored in physics at university.

3) We are still in the process of moving house.

4) She seems to do these things on purpose.

5) He suffered terribly with his feet.

Writing Practice

Directions: *This part is to test your ability to do practical writing. You are asked to write a letter to your high school teacher according to the information given below. You should write no less than 120 words.*

Sample

1) Tianjin, China
November 16, 2006

2) Mr. Li Weifeng

Zhengzhou No. 2 Middle School

Zhengzhou 450000

P. R. C.

3) Dear Mr. Li,

4)   How are you! I am writing to you from Tianjin. How are you getting on with your work? I am sure you are very busy. Please take good care of yourself.

    I have been for about two and a half months. However, I still can't adapt myself to the college circumstances. Life at college is quite different from that in high school.

    At college, we have fewer lessons and more free time. Most of the students spend their time studying by themselves in the library or somewhere else, but some students don't know how to arrange their time and they often idle away their valuable time.

    We, six girl students, from different parts of our country, share one dormitory. So when we speak to each other, our different local accents always make us laugh. We live and study together, and it's a very special experience for me.

    Most interesting of all, we have no fixed classrooms as we did in high school. After class, we have to look for a classroom to study in.

    I think the most important thing at college is that we should make full use of time and learn as much knowledge as possible. I believe I can make great progress at college.

    Best wishes!

5) Yours sincerely,

6) Wang Ying

(220 words)

英文书信通常由六个部分组成：

1) 信头(Heading)；

2）收信人的姓名与地址（Inside Name and Address）；

3）称呼（Salutation）；

4）正文（Body of the letter）；

5）结束语（Complimentary Close）；

6）署名（Signature）。

如果有附言（Postscript—P. S. ）或附件（Enclosure—Encl），则在信后加上。

Further Practice

Part 1   Multiple Choice

Directions：*There are 10 incomplete sentences in this part. For each sentence there are four choices marked **A**, **B**, **C** and **D**. Choose the **ONE** that best completes the sentence.*

1~5　B　A　D　C　D　　　　6~10　A　B　D　C　C

Part 2   Cloze

Directions：*Fill in the blanks with the proper prepositions or adverbs.*

（1）to　　　　（2）with　　　（3）up　　　（4）as　　　　（5）of

（6）of　　　　（7）with　　　（8）to　　　（9）in　　　　（10）of

Part 3   Reading Comprehension

Directions：*Choose the best answer after reading the following passage.*

1~5　C　B　D　A　D

Key & Difficult Points：(重点、难点)

New Words

honor，miss，offer，manage，pack，accident，pretty，imply，informal，simply，impolite，impression，handsome，smart，scholarship，urban，giant，confident，encourage，challenge，departure，literature

Phrases & Expressions

drink to，give sb. a hand，be full of oneself，prefer to，get to know，in this way，get acquainted with，grow up，regard as，get rid of，be responsible for，accuse of，"it"作形式宾语的用法，accept 与 receive 的区别，反义疑问句的用法，助动词"do"用于肯定句中起强调作用的用法。

Exercises

Listening Practice：Section B(Exercise)
Reading Practice： **Text A**   Part 2   Words & Structure (Exercise 1)
                 Part 3   Translation (Exercise 2)
           Text B   Part 2   Words & Structure (Exercise 1, 2)
                 Part 3   Translation (Exercise 2)
Writing Practice
Further Practice：Part 1   Multiple Choice
                  Part 2   Cloze

Listening Practice

Section A

Key to

Exercise 1

Directions: *Listen to a passage and answer the following questions with* **ONE** *word in each blank.*

1. A. intimate
   B. personal
   C. social
   D. public
2. Culture

Exercise 2

Directions: *Listen to the passage again and choose the best answer.*

1~3   A   D   C

Tape-script

Communication

In interpersonal communication, people in almost every culture recognize four different distances: intimate, personal, social and public. Intimate distance occurs in a very close relationship such as between a mother and a child. Personal distance lets good friends talk closely but comfortably. Social distance is used at parties or other gatherings. Public distance concerns more formal situations such as between a teacher and a student.

These four types of distance exist in all countries, but the amount of distance usually depends on the culture. At a party, for example, a Canadian may sit several feet away from you, while an Arab may sit very near to you. Your awareness of the other culture's use of distance can often help you communicate better with its people.

Section B

Key to

Exercise

Directions: *Listen to a passage and fill in the blanks.*

1. useful and important
2. feels good
3. do better
4. down-hearted
5. children
6. more active
7. leaders and the masses
8. pleasant

Tape-script

Try to Praise Others

Praise is very useful and important to a person. When a person has done something good and is praised, he feels good. Praise may bring his initiative into full play, so he can do better and contribute more in the future. On the contrary, a person may feel down-hearted when he has done something good and not received praise.

The effect of praise is even greater to children. Studies have shown that a child will become more active when he is praised.

Try to praise others in your everyday life. It can promote understanding between leaders and the masses. It can ease the tension among colleagues and neighbors. Too much complaining and criticism will do the opposite. So we should learn to praise others and help to create a light, pleasant atmosphere in which we live.

Oral Practice

对话 1

情景

美国人喜欢周末聚会,江先生和太太在美国工作,艾莉是他们的好朋友。今天星期六,所以艾莉邀请他们共进晚餐。

艾莉：　　　请随便坐。今晚我们准备好了中国餐。希望你们会喜欢。

先生：　　　一定。听起来很好吃。

太太：　　　再次在此相聚太好了。

艾莉：　　　你们能来我觉得很荣幸。江先生和夫人，让我们为你们的健康
　　　　　　干杯！

先生和太太：多谢。

艾莉：　　　这是中国的凉菜。请随便吃。

太太：　　　别担心。我们不会错过任何好吃的。

先生：　　　你把醋递给我好吗，艾莉？

艾莉：　　　给你。

先生：　　　谢谢。

先生和太太：哦，恐怕时间不早了。我们该走了。艾莉，谢谢你的款待。晚安！

艾莉：　　　非常感谢你们的到来。晚安。

对话 2

情景

　　　漂亮姑娘格雷丝带着个大箱子正在路上缓慢地行走，这时，年轻小伙
波比走上前去主动提出要帮格雷丝拿东西。

波：嗨，要我帮忙吗？

格：我就想快点到我车上。

波：我正好顺路。

格：我母亲告诉过我，千万不要接受陌生人的帮助。

波：我叫波比。听到了吧？我们不再是陌生人了。你看这有多么容易，美人？

格：你能不能别这样叫我？

波：可我不知道你的名字。

格：也许我并不想让你知道。（停下来）

波：要是你不想的话，也许你就不会停下来了。

格：你太自以为是了。

波：我喜欢你对我的评价。

格：我叫格雷丝。

波：格雷丝，让我替你拿行李好吗？（格雷丝把箱子递给他。）哇，还蛮重的。

格：你的手怎么了？

波：出了点小事故。

格：你可要当心一些。（波比把箱子放到格雷丝的吉普车上。）谢谢你，波比。

波：别客气，格雷丝。

格：你不是本地人，对吧？

波：我今天早上刚到这儿。我的车在路上开锅了。

格：幸好它没有在沙漠里开锅。否则，像这样的天气，你很快就会被晒死的。

Reading Practice

Text A

美国人的致意方式

美国人时常只是用"哈罗"或"嗨"来彼此打招呼。他们认为这种比较随意的问候能表示一种亲密而友好的关系。同样，美国人没有正式的"辞别"。他们一般只是挥挥手向大家"告别"；也许他们只说一句"再见"，"回见吧"或"说到时间，我得赶紧跑了"就算告辞。对美国人来说，友好且随意的关系是最重要的。

是的，适当的介绍将会给人留下美好的第一印象。然而美国式的介绍通常相当简单。在美国，大多数人作介绍时不喜欢使用"先生"、"太大"或"小姐"等称呼。他们觉得这种称谓太古板。比起正式称呼，大部分情形下他们更喜欢直呼其名。举例来说，一位先生可能说"见到你很高兴。我姓米勒。但叫我保罗好了。"有时一位初次见面的女士可能说"不必叫我史密斯太太，就叫我莎莉吧"。所以如果你的美国朋友没有称呼你的姓氏或头衔，你不必觉得他们失礼。他们不过是想要表示友好。

当你初次结识一个美国人时，他可能问你："你在哪里工作呢？""你结婚了吗？"或"你有孩子吗？"这种问题对欧洲人来说可能太涉及个人隐私了。但是美国人有时确实会问此类问题。他们想要得到你对这些询问的回答，这样就能更多地了解你，并以此为开端与你友好地侃上一场。

Exercises

Part 1　Reading Comprehension

1. Directions：*Complete each of the following statements according to the text.*

1) use Mr. , Mrs. And Miss

2) use first names

3) call me Sally

4) glad/happy

5) informal/friendly

2. Directions: *Answer the following questions according to the text.*

1) It means a close and friendly relationship.

2) They find these terms too formal.

3) They only want to show their friendliness.

4) They want to know more about you so that they can begin a talk with you.

Part 2　Words and Structure

1. Directions: *Match an expression in **Column B** which is similar in meaning to the one in **Column A**.*

1)~5)　d　f　i　h　b　　　　6)~10)　j　a　c　g　e

2. Directions: *Choose the correct meaning for the italicized words.*

1)~5)　B　B　A　B　A

Part 3　Translation

1. Directions: *Translate the following passage into Chinese.*

1) 他们认为这种比较随意的问候能表示一种亲密而友好的关系。

2) 比起正式称呼,大部分情形下他们更喜欢直呼其名。

3) 所以如果你的美国朋友没有称呼你的姓氏或头衔,你不必觉得他们失礼。

4) 这种问题对欧洲人来说可能太涉及个人隐私了。但是美国人有时确实会问此类问题。

5) 这样就能更多地了解你,并以此为开端与你友好地侃上一场。

2. Directions: *Translate the following sentences into English.*

1) Farewell! I hope we meet again soon.

2) It was impolite of her not to say goodbye.

3) On her small income they live very simply.

4) Her speech made quite an impression on the audience.

5) Men must wear a jacket and tie, similarly, women must wear a skirt or dress, not trousers.

Text B

参考译文

天 生 输 家
部分电影简介

保罗是在一个小镇上长大的。他英俊、聪明、善良，在当地很受人们的喜爱。通过自己的努力，他终于取得了纽约大学的全额奖学金。但是到这样的大城市去与见多识广的城市孩子一起学习让保罗感到有些忐忑不安。在为他举行的送别晚会上，保罗的父亲鼓励他面对新生活的挑战。他告诉保罗，感兴趣是成为有趣的人的前提，也就是说如果你肯倾听别人，他们就会把你当朋友看。记着这番话，保罗来到了纽约大学。他发现这儿的大多数学生都很自私，他们只对自己感兴趣。

上文学课时，几个学生用恶作剧捉弄保罗，使他从报告厅的台阶上跌了下去，这引起了同学们的哄堂大笑。当他找了个座位坐下来时，邻座的一个漂亮女孩试着用可乐杯里的冰块为他膝盖上的伤镇痛，保罗深受感动。

保罗一直在用功学习以保持他的全额奖学金。而他的三个室友却老是去聚会狂欢、享受生活。他们还取笑保罗土里土气的穿着以及"只知用功不会娱乐"的态度，说没有人会喜欢保罗的。他们很不喜欢他，打算把他赶走。所以，他们到宿舍管理委员会控告保罗既不做值日又不讲个人卫生，这真是信口雌黄。保罗其实也不愿和他们住在一块，所以他同意搬出来。但由于宿舍紧张，他只好搬到动物诊所的值班室，同时负责夜间照看动物。因为过去几个月里室友不务正业的折腾造成的干扰，保罗无法集中精力学习，结果文学课的期中成绩只得了个 B。这就意味着他必须以后努力学习才能保住下学期的奖学金。

Exercises

Part 1   Reading Comprehension

Direction: Decide whether the following statements are true or false according to the text. Write "**_T_**" *for True and* "**_F_**" *for False.*

1)～5) F T F T F   6)～10) F T T F T

Part 2   Words and Structure

1. Directions: *Match an expression in* **Column B** *which is similar in meaning to the* **ONE** *in* **Column A**.

1)~5)   i   h   d   g   a   6)~10)   j   c   e   b   f

2. Directions: *Fill in each of the blanks with an appropriate word from the box. Change the form if necessary.*

1) with   2) up

3) as   4) accused

5) for   6) among

Part 3   Translation

1. Directions: *Translate the following passage into Chinese.*

　　保罗是在一个小镇上长大的。他英俊、聪明、善良,在当地很受人们的喜爱。通过自己的努力,他终于取得了纽约大学的全额奖学金。但是到这样的大城市去与见多识广的城市孩子一起学习让保罗感到有些忐忑不安。在为他举行的送别晚会上,保罗的父亲鼓励他面对新生活的挑战。他告诉保罗,感兴趣是成为有趣的人的前提,也就是说如果你肯倾听别人,他们就会把你当朋友看。

2. Directions: *Translate the following sentences into English.*

1) Thank you for your kind hospitality.

2) Please give your introductions.

3) The patient is comfortable after his operation.

4) I only found it by accident.

5) His behavior is impolite.

Writing Practice

Directions: *For this part , you are asked to write a composition on the topic :* "**How to Establish a Good First Impression**?" *You should write at least 120 words according to the suggestions given below in Chinese.*

Sample

How to Establish a Good First Impression?

It is said that first impressions are lasting impressions. People form opinions and make judgments about us the first time they see or hear us. And these opinions cannot be changed easily later.

Unfavorable impressions can be damaging results. For example, if you are a salesman and have left a bad first impression on your customer, he will probably refuse to buy your product. Create a good first impression and the relationship grows from there. Create a bad first impression and your relationship with that person can be an uphill battle.

Then how to leave a good impression on others? First and foremost, good manners are essential. Being polite and friendly with others will help you earn their favor. And it's also important that your appearance in clean and neat. They nay you can't judge a book by its cover but how many of us make judgments about people just based on their appearance?

(154 words)

Further Practice

Part 1　Multiple choice

Directions: *There are 10 incomplete sentences in this part. For each sentence there are four choices marked **A**, **B**, **C** and **D**. Choose the **ONE** that best completes the sentence.*

1~5 A C C A D 　　6~10 D C D B D

Part 2　Cloze

Directions: *There are 10 blanks in the following passage. For each blank there are four choices marked A, B and C. Choose the **ONE** that best fits into the passage.*

1~5 A A C B A 　　6~10 B C C B C

Part 3　Reading Comprehension

Directions:*Choose the best answer after reading the following passage.*
1～5　D　C　C　C　C

Unit 3 *Study*

Key & Difficult Points：(重点、难点)

New Words

hobby, expensive, calm, depressed, draft, information, utter, connect, soul, conscious, faith, genius, devotion, intimate, constantly, combine, appreciate, contend, vibration, fault, achievement, announce, silly, mail, dumb, taste, mention, advance

Phrases & Expressions

take a picture, in one's spare time, be fond of, take it easy, but for, in one's efforts (to do), call one's attention, look forward to (doing) sth., cast sb. down, by the time, graduate from, burst into, at random, 现在分词作伴随状语的用法。

Exercises

Listening Practice：Section A(Exercise 1，2)
Reading Practice：**Text A**　Part 1　Reading Comprehension (Exercise 1，2)
　　　　　　　　　　　　Part 2　Words & Structure (Exercise 1，2)
　　　　　　　　　　　　Part 3　Translation (Exercise 2)
　　　　　　　　Text B　Part 1　Reading Comprehension (Exercise 1)
　　　　　　　　　　　　Part 2　Words & Structure (Exercise 2)
Writing Practice
Further Practice：Part 1　Multiple Choice

Listening Practice

Key to

Exercise 1

Directions: *In this section, you will hear 5 short conversations. At the end of each conversation, a question will be asked about what was said. Listen carefully and choose the best answer.*

1~5   A C B C A

Tape-script

1. M: Yes, I would like that pair of trousers sized 9. I'll take it.

   W: OK, the color is good on you, and if you feel it uncomfortable, you can come to exchange within three days.

   Q: What is the possible relationship between the two speakers?

2. M: Would you like to go dancing with me this evening, Susan? We seldom have had any time together recently.

   W: I really would like to. But the preparations for the final exams have kept me busy. Maybe we can go at weekend.

   Q: What are the woman going to do after dinner?

3. W: How much is the rent of the apartment?

   M: It's a hundred and fifty dollars a month unfurnished or two hundred dollars a month furnished. Utilities are twenty-five dollars extra.

   Q: How much will it cost the man to rent an unfurnished department, including utilities?

4. M: Did you get what you wanted? You've been out all the afternoon.

   W: I looked all over the district, and I didn't find any dress interesting to me, and they are so expensive.

   Q: What can we learn about the woman?

5. M: Are you busy Friday night? If not, would you like to go to the concert?

   W: I have a few commitments. But I think I can postpone them for another time.

Q: What will the woman probably do?

Exercise 2

Directions: *In this section, you will hear a passage. At the end of the passage, there are some questions. Listen carefully and choose the best answer.*

1~5 A C B A D

Tape-script

Learners of English

Learners of English, especially self-taught learners may have trouble in understanding speeches by native speakers. The following ways might help improve their listening ability.

First of all, do things step by step. It is not good to listen to something beyond your level. Better choose a suitable course and start with the first book. Go on to the second book only after you are sure you understand the first one.

Secondly, stick to one course of study. Don't change books often. Never let your attention be attracted by another course just because it seems to be more "fashionable".

Thirdly, listen to the English news program over the radio from time to time. Better go through the news stories in the Chinese-language newspaper first. That will make it easier for you to understand the English news on the radio.

Fourthly, if you have time, listen to some interesting stories in "Special English from the V. O. A." or other listening materials of the same level as that of your textbook.

Section B

Key to

Exercise 1

Directions: *In this section, you will hear a passage. At the end of the passage,*

26

there are some statements. Decide whether they are true or false.
Write "T" for true and "F" for false in the space provided.

1~5   T   T   F   T   F

Exercise 2

Directions: *Listen to the passage again and answer the following questions.*

1. The advice is to learn with good methods and practice with a purpose.
2. We should listen to English tapes, radio and TV programs, and even to ourselves.
3. Because you can listen to your own voice and compare your pronunciation with that of the

speakers' on the tape.

4. We should pay attention not only to our pronunciation and intonation, but also to the meaning of

what we're reading.

5. Because making mistakes means we're making progress.

Tape-script

Practice Makes Perfect

Good morning, boys and girls. Today I'll answer some questions you asked last week about English study. As to how to do listening and speaking practice, I think you can start with listening, then repeat or imitate what you've heard, and then speak. You can listen to English tapes, radio and TV programs, and even to yourself. After listening you should imitate by reading aloud. You can tape your voice and then listen to it again, to compare your pronunciation with that of the speakers' on the tape. One more thing to remind you, when you're reading aloud, you should pay attention not only to your pronunciation and intonation, but also to the meaning of what you're reading. You can do it alone or together with your classmates. Usually we don't like to do it in public, because we are afraid of losing face. Oh, remember, boys and girls, everyone makes mistakes when learning English, and I think making mistakes means you're making progress. So my advice is to learn with good methods and practice with a purpose. If you make English learning fun, you're already half way there.

Oral Practice

对话 1

情景

约翰和迈克是新同学,他们彼此不太了解。但是,第一次见面都留下了好印象,并想尽快成为好朋友。下面是他们俩的谈话:

约翰:迈克,你的爱好是什么?

迈克:哦,我喜欢音乐和摄影。

约翰:但爱好摄影是件很花钱的事,对吗?

迈克:是的,我想你说得对。业余时间你喜欢做什么?

约翰:我喜欢钓鱼和狩猎。夏天,我最喜欢游泳。

迈克:你打网球吗?

约翰:打,但打得不太好。我打网球只是为了娱乐而已。

迈克:我们以后有时一起玩好吗?

约翰:好,很好。我们定在下周吧。

迈克:就这么定了。

对话 2

情景

期末临近,约翰担心他的最后考试,整日情绪低落。他的好朋友迈克过来安慰他并提出些建议。

迈克:约翰,怎么了? 你看上去很沮丧。

约翰:我担心星期五的考试。

迈克:泰然处之吧。不必为它担忧。我相信如果你保持冷静,你会做好的。

约翰:我只是不知道考试时能否使用电子词典。

迈克:我想不能。

约翰:如果我考试中有问题能问老师吗?

迈克:恐怕那是不可能的。

约翰：那么我可以带些纸打草稿吗？

迈克：可以，没关系。

约翰：非常感谢你告诉我这些。

Reading Practice

Text A

Pre-reading

有时我想，把每天都当作生命的最后一天来度过也不失为一个很好的生命法则。这种人生态度使人非常重视人生的价值。每一天我们都应该以和善的态度、充沛的精力和热情的欣赏来度过，而这些恰恰是在来日方长时往往被我们忽视的东西。

——海伦·凯勒

参考译文

我是怎样学说话的

海伦·凯勒

我永远也忘不了，当我第一次说出"天气很暖和"这个完整的句子时有多么惊喜。诚然，它们只是一些断断续续、结结巴巴的音节，但这毕竟是人类的语言。我感觉得到有一股新的力量，为我挣脱了灵魂的枷锁，通过这些断续的语言符号，带我向知识和一切信念前进。

但是，千万不要以为在这短短的时间内，我就真地能说话了。我只是掌握了一些语言的要素。虽然富勒小姐和沙莉文小姐能听懂我的意思，不过多数人还是难得听明白。而且，也不要以为，在掌握了这些语言要素之后，我就可以靠自己逐步完成学习。要是没有沙莉文小姐的天才与她孜孜不倦的热忱，我是无法达到自然的言谈的。起初，我不分昼夜地苦练，才使我最亲近的朋友能够听懂我的发音；继而，在莎莉文小姐的帮助下，我坚持不懈地反复练习发准每一个音节以及各种各样的音节组合。直到今天，她还是每天提醒我，纠正我不正确的发音。

所有失聪儿童的教师都知道这意味着什么，也只有他们才能体会到我所必须克服的是怎样的困难。我不得不通过手指的触摸来感觉老师讲话时喉咙的颤动、嘴唇的动作和面部的表情,而感觉往往又不准确。这样,我就得反复练习那些单词或句子,有时要练上几个小时、直到感觉自己的发音准确了为止。我的任务就是练习、练习、再练习。失败和疲惫常让我心怀沮丧,可一想到很快就要回家,能让我所爱的人看到我的进步,我就又有了动力。我一心期望让他们为我的成功而欢喜欣慰。

Exercises

Part 1　Reading Comprehension

1. Directions: *Decide whether the statements are true or false according to the text. Write "**T**" for true and "**F**" for false in the space provided.*

1)～5)　T　F　T　T　F

2. Directions: *Fill in the blanks with the proper words according to the text.*

(1) uttered　　　　　　2) speech

(3) symbol　　　　　　(4) to

(5) not　　　　　　　　(6) elements

(7) natural　　　　　　(8) untiring perseverance

(9) devotion(10) labored

(11) constantly(12) peculiar

(13) contended(14) Discouragement

(15) pleasure

3. Directions: *Answer the following questions according to the text.*

1) It was "It is warm".

2) All teachers of the deaf.

3) She had to use the sense of touch in catching the vibrations of the throat, the movements of the mouth and the expression of the face; and often the sense was at fault. She was forced to repeat the words or sentences, sometimes for hours, until she felt the proper ring in her own voice.

Part 2　Words & Structure

1. Directions: *Match an expression in **Column B** which is similar in meaning to the one in **Column A**.*

1)～5)　b　c　a　d　i　　　　6)～10)　e　j　f　h　g

2. Directions: *Fill in each of the blanks with an appropriate word from the box.*
               Change the form if necessary.

1) forced   2) devoted

3) eagerness   4) mispronounced

5) intimation   6) labor

Part 3　Translation

1. Directions: *Translate the following passage into Chinese.*

海伦·凯勒

    海伦·凯勒出生时是个正常、健康的孩子。一岁时,她发高烧,得了一场重病。从此,海伦永远失去了视力和听觉。

    幼年时的海伦性格暴躁、孤僻。但她6岁时,发生了一件可喜的事情,她父母为她请了一位老师。他们请了一位年轻的家庭教师——安妮·沙莉文,来帮助海伦学习。海伦经过艰苦努力,开始学习手语了。安教会海伦很多重要的东西,比如怎样像别的孩子那样懂礼貌、守规矩。海伦聪明伶俐,学东西很快。她学会了用盲文阅读。8岁时,她出名了。人们看到她能做那么多事情感到非常惊讶。

    海伦继续学习。20岁时,她进入大学。海伦在大学期间学习极其优秀,以至一家杂志出钱请她写自传。大学毕业后,她决定以写作和讲演的方式谋生。她走遍世界各地,为开办盲人、聋哑人的专门学校和图书馆而辛勤工作。她著书很多,其中一本是写她的老师安妮·沙莉文。

2. Directions: *Translate the following sentences into English.*

1) I read your new book with real delight.

2) She does not appreciate good wine.

3) My grandparents are rather ancient.

4) He never uttered a word of protest.

5) Teenagers are very fashion conscious.

6) She turned a deaf ear to our warnings and got lost.

7) Success was achieved by the combined efforts of the whole team.

8) I am a little deaf, please articulate clearly.

9) Of course, I won't leave you alone, you silly.

10) He has tasted the soup.

Text B

参考译文

我不懂写作

15 岁的时候,我对班上同学宣布说准备写书,并自己画插图。一半的学生开始窃笑,其余的则几乎从椅子上笑得跌到地上。"别傻了,只有天才才能成为作家,"英文老师自以为是地说道,"而你这个学期只有可能得 D。"我羞愧得大哭起来。

那天晚上,我写了一首关于梦想破灭的伤心短诗,并将它寄给了《卡普里周报》。出乎意料的是,他们发表了这首小诗并给我寄来了两美元。我是作家了,我的作品发表了并因此而得到了报酬。我拿给老师和同学看,他们都笑我。"瞎猫逮着死耗子,"老师说道。我尝到了成功的甜头。我的第一篇作品就卖出去了。这比他们任何人做得都强,如果这是瞎猫逮着死耗子,那么我不在乎。

在接下来的两年里,我卖掉了几十首诗歌、书信、笑话和食谱。中学毕业时,我的平均成绩是 C+,但我的剪贴簿里已经贴满了我发表的作品。我再也没有将自己的写作情况告诉老师、同学或家人。他们都是无情的摧梦者。

现时我有四个孩子,最大的只有四岁。孩子们进入梦乡时,我就在那台老掉牙的打字机前打字,我写下自己的感受。这花了我九个月的时间,就像十月怀胎。我随意选择了一家出版社寄了出去。

一个月后,我收到一份合同、一份预付款和特许权以及另一本书的约稿。这本名为《哭泣的风》的书成了畅销的书,并被译成 15 国文字和盲文,销往世界各地。我的第一本书被列为加拿大本土美语学校的必读课程。

人们问我曾上过什么大学,得过什么学位,获过什么资格证书才成为作家。答案是:"什么也没有。"我只是写。我不是天才。我并没有写作天分也不懂写作。

对于那些梦想写作的人,我想大喊一声:"行的,你一定能行。不要听信别人。"我不懂写作,可是我战胜了不可能。写作很容易,十分有趣,每个人都做得来。当然,哪怕是瞎猫逮着死耗子也无关紧要。

Exercises

Part 1   Reading Comprehension

1. Directions: *Decide whether the statements are true or false according to the* *text. Write "**T**" for true and "**F**" for false in the space provided.*

1)~5)　T　F　T　F　F

2. Directions：*Answer the following questions according to the text.*

1) She announced that she was going to write and illustrate her own books.

2) Because she was so humiliated.

3) She sold dozens of poems, letters, jokes and recipes.

4) No.

5) Writing is easy, it's fun and anyone can do it. Of course, a little dumb luck doesn't hurt. Her success shows us a fact - whatever you do, as long as you work hard and never give up, you'll be a winner someday.

Part 2　Words & Structure

1. Directions：*Match an expression in **Column B** which is similar in meaning to the one in **Column A**.*

1)~5)　e　g　j　c　b　　　　6)~10)　i　h　d　a　f

2. Directions：*Fill in each of the blanks with an appropriate word or phrase from the box. Change the form if necessary.*

1) qualified　　　　　　　2) royalties

3) nap　　　　　　　　　4) dumb luck

5) random　　　　　　　　6) astonished

Part 3　Translation

1. Directions：*Translate the following sentences into Chinese.*

1) 一半的学生开始窃笑,其余的则几乎从椅子上笑得跌到地上。

2) 我羞愧得大哭起来。

3) 这比他们任何人做得都强,如果这是瞎猫逮着死耗子,那么我不在乎。

4) 我随意选择了一家出版社寄了出去。

5) 写作很容易,十分有趣,每个人都做得来。当然,哪怕是瞎猫逮着死耗子也无关紧要。

2. Directions：*Translate the following sentences into English.*

1) It happened on two successive days.

2) The Grand Hotel is playing host to this year's sales conference.

3) You have to get official permission to build a new house.

4) In the last five years the city has spread out rapidly in all directions.

5) I have been offered a job to Japan.

6) It must have been a political decision.

7) The brothers look very similar.

8) His second novel established his fame as a writer.

9) Routine office jobs have no relish at all for me.

10) He immersed himself totally in his work.

Writing Practice

Directions: *For this part, you are asked to write a composition on the topic:*
"Learning English Is Not So Easy". You should write at least 120
words according to the suggestions given below in Chinese.

Sample

Learning English Is Not So Easy

As an ad says, "Learning English in three months, or your money back!" Of course, it never happens quite like that. If it is true, it will save the learners a lot of time and energy. As we know, no language is easy to learn, including one's mother tongue.

English, as a language, has its difficult points to learn. For example, there are so many idioms in English. Another example is the spelling. Learners have to spend a lot of time learning them by heart. And they must put practice into the first place. The more you practice, the more you benefit. So English learners are required to speak more and read more. English becomes easy only in practice.

Some people say it is easy to learn English in the United Stats, England or Canada. This may be true. But most learners cannot afford to study abroad. They can learn English from their teachers. Besides, modern science and technology provide good means for learning languages. Tape recorders, radios,

34

television and computers will help. In a word, in order to learn English well, learners have a lot of thing to do.

(191 words)

Further Practice

Part 1   Multiple choice

Directions: *There are 10 incomplete sentences in this part. For each sentence there are four choices marked* **A, B, C** *and* **D.** *Choose the* **ONE** *that best completes the sentence.*

1~5   C   C   A   B   D   6)~10)   A   C   B   D   A

Part 2   Cloze

Directions: *There are 10 blanks in the following passage. For each blank there are four choices marked* **A, B, C** *and* **D.** *Choose the* **ONE** *that best fits into the passage.*

 1~5   A   D   B   B   C   6~10   D   C   C   B   A
11~15   D   A   C   D   A   16-20   D   B   B   C   A

Part 3   Reading Comprehension

Directions: *Answer the 5 questions after reading the following passage. Just write a word or a phrase for each answer.*

1. To introduce some skills for reading comprehension.
2. To improve your comprehension.
3. Survey.
4. Scanning.
5. Skimming.

Key & Difficult Points：(重点、难点)

New Words

channel, ordinary, network, local, interrupt, opposite, intelligent, propose, prohibit, proposal, generation, communicate, disturb, emotional, pastime, product, electronic, partly, involve, invent, injure, science, adore, alike, argument, settle, appearance

Phrases & Expressions

a set of, because of, not... until, draw up, change into, bring...(to..., turn against, be in debt, in poverty, in part, bring together, come up with, have a ball

Exercises

Listening Practice：Section A (Exercise 1)
Section B (Exercise 1)
Reading Practice：**Text A** Part 2 Words & Structure(Exercise 1, 3)
Part 3 Translation(Exercise 2)
Text B Part 2 Words & Structure (Exercise 2)
Part 3 Translation (Exercise 2)
Writing Practice
Further Practice：Part 1 Multiple Choice
Part 3 Reading Practice

Listening Practice

Section A

Key to

Exercise 1

Directions: *You will hear ten sentences. Each sentence contains one of the two words given to you. Listen carefully and underline the letter beside the word you hear in the sentence.*

1~5 A B B A B   6~10 B A B A B

Tape-script

1. Are the classes large?
2. Do you see the cock over there?
3. Thank you for the gift.
4. Susan felt very hungry after class.
5. Are you waiting for the boss?
6. Rose enjoys working with Ruth.
7. Can you ride well?
8. Has Mr. Bird got a brown cow?
9. I've got a very bad pain.
10. Sam bought his friend a bunch of flowers yesterday.

Exercise 2

Directions: *You will hear ten sentences. Each sentence contains one of the three words given to you. Listen carefully and underline the letter beside the word you hear in the sentence.*

1~5 C B C B C   6~10 A B B C A

Tape-script

1. Is your friend called John?

37

2. They are waiting for their books.

3. Have you seen her lately?

4. Excuse me, can I see Miss Taylor?

5. Pass me the salt, please.

6. Is the man feeling cold?

7. Tom and his wife look very healthy.

8. Peter is always right.

9. This is Bob Smith speaking.

10. Are you going to sell the boat?

Section B

Key to

Exercise 1

Directions: *You're going to hear a passage. At the end of the passage you will hear five questions. Listen carefully and choose the right answer to each question you hear.*

1~4 B A B C C

Exercise 2

Directions: *Listen again and complete the following with the words you hear.*

1. 3463; 3464   2. tired; last   3. 20 minutes

Tape-script

I'm Sorry, You Have the Wrong Number

Mrs. Jones' telephone number was 3463, and the number of the cinema in her town was 3464, so people often made a mistake and telephoned her when they wanted the cinema.

One evening the telephone bell rang and Mrs. Jones answered it. A tired man said, "At what time does your last film begin?"

"I'm sorry," said Mrs. Jones, "but you have the wrong number. This is not the cinema."

"Oh, it began twenty minutes ago," said the man. " I'm sorry about that. Goodbye."

Mrs. Jones was very surprised, so she told her husband. He laughed and said, "The man's wife wanted to go to the cinema, but he was feeling tired, so he telephoned the cinema. His wife heard him, but she didn't hear you. Now they will stay at home this evening, and the husband will be happy!"

1. Why did people often telephone Mrs. Jones when they wanted the cinema?
2. Why was Mrs. Jones so surprised at a phone call one evening?
3. According to Mr. Jones, why didn't the man want to go to the cinema?
4. What do you think the man's wife wanted to do that evening?
5. What do you think of the man who called?

Oral Practice

参考译文

对话 1

情景
    学生甲和乙分别来自不同的国家。学生甲来自中国,学生乙来自美国。他们在同一所大学学习共住一个宿舍。现在电视开着,他们正在一起边看电视边讨论。

甲:我换一个频道好吗? 有人反对吗?

乙:请吧。

甲:哪一个频道是新闻?

乙:开 12 频道试试。

甲:噢,是它。请告诉我,这些频道都是怎么收看的?

乙:如果你有一台一般的电视机,你只能收到本地主要电视频道的节目。

甲:要是您想看看诸如体育之类的节目,怎么办呢?

乙:您可以买有线电视的频道,每一个频道都放映一种专门的节目,如体育、音乐、电影等。

甲：想买多少都行吗？

乙：都可以，中国有有线电视吗？

甲：没有。在大城市，我们能收到两三个频道，在大多数的地方可以收到北京的电视节目。在更大的城市里还可以收到省台或市台的节目，如果这个市自己有电视台的话。

乙：那么电视台都放映什么样的节目？

甲：星期一到星期六的上、下午有教育节目，中午有新闻节目，晚上一般七点是新闻节目，在这之后有电影、电视剧和其他的节目，星期天有电影、歌剧、体育和儿童节目。

乙：您看到了我们的电视广告了，你们也有吗？

甲：我们刚开始有广告，但我们广告的出现从不打断一个节目，而是安排在节目和节目之间进行。

乙：噢，那倒是个好办法，广告真讨厌，我们这样做是因为电视台不能不赚钱，那些公司为了播放广告要付很多钱。

甲：新闻节目完了。好像我得去准备明天的考试了。

乙：噢，我也是，再见。

甲：再见。

对话 2

情景

罗德尼、艾米莉和简是好朋友。现在他们要去球场观看正在举行的足球赛。

罗德尼：咱们进去吧。我什么也听不到，太吵了。

艾米莉：怎么回事？大家都在喊什么？

罗德尼：你看见球场对面的那个样子很丑的人了吗？他是威尔士最棒的球员之一。

艾米莉：控着球的那位吗？

罗德尼：进球！你见过比那个漂亮的球吗？

艾米莉：什么意思？

简：　　威尔士刚进了一个球，琼斯踢进的。

罗德尼：他表现得最好。他最聪明。

简：　　他长相最丑。

艾米莉:现在谁领先？

罗德尼:比分平着呢。英格兰进了一球,威尔士也进了一球。刚才那个球太漂亮了。英格兰今天踢得太差劲了。你瞧一瞧卡特。是这个球队中踢得最差的一个人。

艾米莉:这支球队不是英格兰最好的吗？

简：　　当然是。但今天他们踢得不太好。罗德尼希望英格兰赢这场比赛,所以他不高兴。

艾米莉:为什么？ 两个球队表现得都很好。

简：　　但威尔士刚进了一球。英格兰本应该会赢得这场比赛,但现在看来不行了。两个队都进了一球。

罗德尼:看! 琼斯抢到了球,还有 20 秒钟,但威尔士队又要射门了。球进了! 比赛结束了。他们赢了。

Reading Practice

Text A

参考译文

关上电视:清静一小时

我想建议每天晚上一播完晚间新闻,美国所有的电视台都依法停播 60～90 分钟。

让我们认真而通情达理地看一下:如果这一建议被采纳的话,会有什么样的结果。千家万户也许会利用这段时间真正地团聚一番。没有电视机的干扰,他们晚饭后也许会围坐在一起,当真交谈起来。众所周知,我们的许多问题——事实上是所有的问题,从代沟、高离婚率到某些精神病——至少部分的是由于没能交流思想而引起的。我们谁也不把自己心头的烦恼告诉别人,结果感情上便产生了这样那样的问题。利用这安静的、全家聚在一起的时刻来讨论我们的各种问题,我们相互之间也许会更加了解,更加相爱。

有些晚上,如果没有必要进行这种交谈,那么各家各户也许会重新发现一些更为积极的消遣活动。如果他们挣脱开电视机的束缚而不得不另寻自己的活动,他们也许会合家驱车去看日落。或者也许全家一起去散步(还记得长有双脚吗?),

用新奇的目光观察住处的周围地区。

有了空闲时间而有没有电视可看，大人小孩便可能重新发现阅读。一本好书里的乐趣，胜过一个月中所有典型的电视节目。教育家们在研究报告中指出，伴随着电视长大的这一代人几乎写不出一句英语句子，甚至受过大学教育的人们也是如此。写作往往是通过阅读学会的。每晚清静一小时，可以造就出文化程度较高的一代新人。

也许还可以像过去那样进行另一种形式的阅读：高声朗读。没有多少娱乐比一家人聚在一起，听爸爸妈妈朗读一篇优美的故事更能使一家人关系融洽和睦了。没有电视干扰的这一小时，可以成为朗读故事的时间。等这静悄悄的一小时过去以后，要想再把我们从新发现的娱乐活动中拉回去，电视联播公司也许将被迫拿出更好的节目来才行。

乍一看，停播一小时电视的想法似乎过于偏激。如果少了这位电子保姆，做父母的可怎么办呢？我们怎么来打发这段时间呢？其实这个想法一点也不偏激。电视开始主宰美国人的空间时间，至今也不过才25年。我们之中那些年满和年过35岁的人，还能回忆起没有电视相伴的童年，那时我们有一部分空间以收音机为伴——听收音机至少还需要发挥听者的想象力——但另外我们还看书、学习、交谈、做游戏、发明一些新的活动。日子也并不那么难过。那时我们确实过得挺开心。

Exercises

Part 1　Reading Comprehension

1. Directions：*Choose the best answer for each of the following items according to the text.*

1)~4)　B　C　D　D　　　　5)~8)　A　C　C　B

2. Directions：*Answer the following questions according to the text.*

1) The author proposes that 60 to 90 minutes each evening right after the early evening news, all television broadcasting in the United States be prohibited by law.

2) If families used a quiet hour to discuss their problems, they might get to know each other better, and to like each other better.

3) Reading.

4) All the family members gather around and listening to mother or father read a

good story. The quiet hour could become the story hour.

5) The advantages of turning off TV for an hour every night are：

(1) People might get to know each other better, and to like each other better.

(2) People are forced to find their own activities, for example, to take a ride together to watch the sunset, to take a walk together (remember feet?) and see the neighborhood with fresh, new eyes.

(3) Children and adults might rediscover reading. A more literate new generation could be a product of the quiet hour.

(4) The quiet hour could become the story hour. Few pastimes bring a family closer together than gather around and listening to mother or father read a good story.

Part 2　Words and Structure

1. Directions： *Choose the definition from* **Column B** *that best matches each italicized word or phrase in* **Column A.**

1)~6)　f　b　k　a　c　d　　　7)~12)　h　i　l　e　j　g

2. Directions： *Give the opposite of the following words.*

1) busy 　　　　2) excluding 　　　3) unreal/imaginary　4) same

5) success 　　　6) unreasonable 　7) noisy 　　　　8) inactive/passive

9) unnecessary 　10) illiterate 　11) dishonest 　　12) dislike

3. Directions： *Fill in each of the blanks with an appropriate word or phrase from the box. Change the form if necessary.*

1) involves 　2) get to 　3) prohibited　4) freed from　5) had caused

6) disturbed 　7) including 　8) come up with　9) come to　10) communicate

Part 3　Translation

1. Directions： *Translate the following sentences into Chinese.*

1)我想建议每天晚上一播完晚间新闻,美国所有的电视台都依法停播 60~90 分钟。

2)众所周知,我们的许多问题——事实上是所有的问题,从代沟、高离婚率到某些精神病——至少部分地是由于没能交流思想而引起的。

3)有些晚上,如果没有必要进行这种交谈,那么各家各户也许会重新发现一些更为积极的消遣活动。

4）如果他们挣脱开电视机的束缚而不得不另寻自己的活动，他们也许会合家驱车去看日落。

5）没有多少娱乐比一家人聚在一起，听爸爸妈妈朗读一篇优美的故事更能使一家人关系融洽和睦了。

6）等这静悄悄的一小时过去以后，要想再把我们从新发现的娱乐活动中拉回去，电视联播公司也许将被迫拿出更好的节目来才行。

2. Directions：*Translate the following sentences into English.*

1）To take this job would involve work on weekends frequently.

2）It is well know that lung cancer is caused at least in part by smoking too much.

3）Few pastimes bring more pleasure to the old man than telling stories to children.

4）I propose that we invite Prof. Smith to our English party tomorrow evening.

5）The committee is made up of eight people，including two women.

6）I hope that you can come up with a better solution than this.

Text B

参考译文

丹尼尔·门杜萨

两百多年前，拳击比赛在英国非常盛行。在那些日子里，拳击家赤手相斗，以获取奖金。因此，他们被称为"职业拳击家"。然而，当时拳击非常粗野，因为没有规则，在比赛中职业拳击家可能受重伤，甚至被打死。

拳击史上最引人注目的人物之一是丹尼尔·门杜萨，他生于1764年。直到1860年昆斯伯里侯爵制定出第一套规则才使用拳击手套。门杜萨虽然就技术而论是一位职业拳击家，但他为把粗鲁的职业拳击变为一项运动作了不少贡献，因为他把科学引进了这项运动。门杜萨一生享有极高的声誉。穷人和富人崇敬他。

年仅14岁的门杜萨参加了一次拳击比赛之后就很快出了名。这引起了当时英国最杰出的拳击家查里德·汉弗来斯的注意。他提出对门杜萨进行培训，而这个年轻的门徒一学就会。事实上，门杜萨很快就成绩斐然，结果汉弗来斯成了他的反对者。他们两人激烈争吵。显然只有通过格斗才能解决这场争吵。比赛在斯蒂尔顿举行,他们格斗了一个小时。公众为门杜萨下了大笔赌注,可是他被击败了。后来门杜萨又一次在拳击场同汉弗来斯较量,结果再次败北。直到 1790 年在第三次比赛中,他才最终击败了汉弗来斯而成为英国的冠军。与此同时,他建立了一个极为成功的拳击学校,甚至拜伦勋爵都成了他的学生。他赚了许多钱,仅仅露一次面他就能获得 100 英镑。尽管如此,但他挥霍无度,总是债台高筑。他在被一个叫"杰克逊绅士"的拳击家击败之后,很快就被人遗忘了。由于还不起债,他就被投进了监狱,并在贫困潦倒之中于 1836 年死去。

Exercises

Part 1 Reading Comprehension

1. Directions:*Give short answers to these questions in your own words According to the text. Use one complete sentence for each answer.*

1) It was because they fought for a prize.

2) It was crude because there were no rules to follow and a boxer could be seriously injured or even killed during the match.

3) He drew up the first set of rules for boxing.

4) He was sent to prison for failing to pay his debts.

2. Directions:*Choose the best answer according to the text*

1)~6) B D C A A B   7)~12) D B B C A D

Part 2 Words & Structure

1. Directions:*Explain the meanings of the following words and phrases as they are used in the passage.*

1) unprotected

2) hurt

3) drafted or prepared

4) rough or not refined

5) was extremely well known and generally liked by the public

6) esteemed

7) in the same way

2. Directions: *Fill in each of the blanks with an appropriate word or phrase from the box. Change the form if necessary.*

1) bare   2) match   3) injured   4) alike   5) adored

6) settle   7) because of   8) drew up   9) changed into 10) bet

Part 3　Translation

1. Directions: *Translate the following sentences into Chinese.*

1)200 年前,拳击比赛在英国非常盛行。

2)当时,拳击手为争夺奖金空手搏斗。

3)因为这样,他们被称为"职业拳击手"。

4)1860 年昆斯伯里多侯爵第一次为拳击比赛制定了规则,拳击比赛这才用上了手套。

5)门多萨在把这种粗鲁的拳击变成一种体育运动方面作出了很大的贡献,因为科学引进了体育运动。

6)事实上,门多萨不久便名声大振,致使汉弗莱斯与他反目为敌。

7)显而易见,只有较量一番才能解决争论。

8)他因无力还债而被捕入狱,于 1836 年在贫困中死去。

2. Directions: *Translate the following sentences into English.*

1) The plan drawn up by our group was adopted at the meeting.

2) Tobacco was introduced into Europe from America.

3) He changed the neat room into a mess.

4) Liberation has brought profound changes to the mountain regions.

5) We all adore our parents.

6) The boy and his father are somewhat alike in appearance.

7) He has turned against his parents.

8) Can you solve the mathematical problem?

9) It was not until Mum came home that she stopped crying.

Writing Practice

Directions: *This part is to test your ability to do practical writing. You are asked to write "A Letter of Invitation*(邀请信)" *according to the* *information given below .*

Sample

August 12, 2006

Dear Meilin,

We have just decided to spend a holiday on the beach this weekend. As we have a spare seat in the car, we think you may be interested in joining us. We remember you said you were fond of sea water bath though you could not swim. Now here's the chance. Besides, we'll do our best to help you learn how to swim. Also, we can take a sunbath together. Please let us know if you would like to go with us and then we'll arrange when to start.

We'll be pleased if you say you can come.

Love,

Joe & Rose

Further Practice

Part 1　Multiple Choice

Directions: *There are 10 incomplete sentences in this part. For each sentence there are four choices marked* **A**, **B**, **C** *and* **D.** *Choose the* **ONE** *that best completes the sentence.*

1~5　C　B　A　B　C　　　　6~10　D　A　A　A　C

Part 2　Cloze

Directions: *There are 20 blanks in this passage, and for each blank there are four choices marked A, B, C, and D at the end of the passage. You should choose the* **ONE** *that best fits into the passage.*

　1~5　D　A　C　B　A　　　　6~10　B　C　A　D　B

11~15　B　C　B　D　C　　　16~20　D　A　C　B　D

Part 3　Reading Comprehension

Directions: *Choose the best answer after reading the following passage.*

1~5　B　C　B　A　B

Unit 5 *Shopping*

Key & Difficult Points：(重点、难点)

New Words

design, perfect, worth, afford, purchase, describe, display, advertisement, impractical, impossible, inefficient, publish, numerous, compete, government, means, define, persuasive, urge, convince, benefit, identify, committee, include

Phrases & Expressions

try on, tell somebody the truth, split the difference, around the clock, be tired of, wait in lines, in front of, range from...to..., turn on, catch one's attention, face to face, aim at, in fact, in this way

Exercises

Listening Practice：Section A (Exercises 1&2)
Section B (Exercise 2)
Reading Practice：**Text A**　Part 2　Words & Structure(Exercise),
　　　　　　　　　　　Part 3　Translation(Exercise)
　　　　　　　　Text B　Part 2　Words & Structure (Exercise),
　　　　　　　　　　　Part 3　Translation (Exercise 2)
Writing Practice
Further Practice：Part 1　Multiple Choice
　　　　　　　　Part 3　Reading Practice

Listening Practice

Section A

Key to

Exercise 1

Directions: *Here are 5 short conversations. Listen to the conversations and choose the best answers to complete the following statements.*

1~5 C A C B B

Tape-script

1. W: Your hat looks nice.

   M: Thank you. It's made of silk.

2. M: Would you please put this lovely watch in a nice box?

   W: Sure.

3. W: You have got three shirts! Is it necessary to buy another one?

   M: But my brother has five shirts.

4. M: How much did your ring cost?

   W: The seller asked for $80. But I got it for half that price.

5. W: I like red and pink most.

   M: My favorite colors are blue and light green.

Exercise 2

Directions: *You will hear ten sentences which contain cardinal numbers. Listen carefully and write down in the brackets the numbers you hear.*

1. 80   2. 2319   3. 7:16   4. 14   5. 15
6. 170   7. 18   8. 1980   9. 3040   10. 13

Tape-script

Exercise 2

1. This silk dress cost Jane 80 dollars.

2. The Porters live at 2319, Main Street.
3. The plane arrived at 7:16 this morning.
4. Hurry up! The train will leave in 14 minutes.
5. The student from Mexico paid 15 pounds for the books.
6. There are 170 girls students in the English Department.
7. It took me 18 minutes to walk to the Shanghai Zoo.
8. John's sister was born in 1980.
9. Mr. Johnson's address is 3040, 2nd Street.
10. Sally was 13 minutes late for class today.

Section B

Key to

Exercise 1

Directions: *Here's a passage. Listen to the passage and then decide whether the following statements are true "T" or false "F".*

1~5 T T F F T

Tape-script

A huge men's shop is having its spring sale. Dad and I come to this shop. We think we'll get some good bargains. We are now in the shirt department. There is a crowd of men waiting to buy shirts. I don't need shirts. I want to buy a new sweater. I've found a sweater I like but it's too expensive. Dad won't allow me to buy an expensive sweater. I have to choose a cheaper one. Oh, here is one. It's only $25. It's a bargain.

Exercise 2   Spot Dictation

Directions: *Here's a short passage. Listen to the passage and fill in the blanks with missing words.*

(1) prefer   (2) offer   (3) variety   (4) reasonable   (5) sales

Tape-script

Students prefer to buy things at campus shops. These shops offer a wide variety of goods for sale from average to better quality products at reasonable prices. These shops prefer a small profit on a great quantity of goods rather than a large profit on fewer sales.

Oral Practice

参考译文

对话 1

> **情景**
>
> 爱丽丝现在一家百货商店。她想买一件羊毛衫。售货员正在给她帮忙。

售货员:下午好,您想买点什么?

艾丽丝:下午好我想买一件羊毛衫。

售货员:我们有许多好羊毛衫。您要买哪一件?

艾丽丝:让我瞧一下 21 号吧。这种设计不错,但是颜色太暗。

售货员:我们还有其他颜色,您要哪种颜色?

艾丽丝:请拿黄色的吧。

售货员:您穿多大的?

艾丽丝:8 号。

售货员:给您。

艾丽丝:我试一试行吗?

售货员:当然可以。

艾丽丝:我穿这件太小,有大一点的吗?

售货员:9 号怎样?

艾丽丝:行,(艾丽丝穿上 9 号羊毛衫。)不错,多少钱?

售货员:328 元。

艾丽丝:不打折吗?

售货员:对不起,不打折。

艾丽丝:好,就要这件吧。

对话 2

情景

菜特太太是一家杂货店的老板,刘小姐到这家杂货店来买花瓶。

刘小姐:　这个花瓶多少钱?

莱特太太:55 美元。

刘小姐:　55 美元? 太贵了。

莱特太太:不贵呀。这个花瓶值 70 美元,因为是最后一个了,我只要 55 美元。

刘小姐:　但已经很旧了。看,这里有点破了。我觉得不值 55 美元,我付你 40 美元。

莱特太太:40 美元? 拜托! 我告诉你,我要 50 美元,50 美元你可以拿走。

刘小姐:　不,还是太贵了。告诉你吧,50 美元我买不起。

莱特太太:对不起,50 美元是最低价了。

刘小姐:　哎,让我们折中一下,45 美元。

莱特太太:45 美元? 好吧,45 美元卖给你了。

刘小姐:　我可以用信用卡付款吗?

莱特太太:可以,小姐。美国特快卡,Visa 卡和万事达卡都可以用。请到收款处
　　　　　付款。

收款员:　给你,请在这里签名。祝你愉快。

刘小姐:　谢谢。也祝你愉快。

Reading Practice

Text A

参考译文

家中购物电视网络

　　你在电视上看过在家里购物的节目吗? 你能描述一下在家里通过电视来购物
的情景吗? 你是否曾经面临过这样的选择:在周末上街采购;还是在家看电视?
如今这两件事你可兼而有之了。家中购物电视网络成了许多人无需走出家门便可

以购物的途径。

　　一些购物者厌倦上商场和购物广场——在人群中挤挤攘攘,排长队等候,甚至有时还买不到想买的东西。他们宁愿静静地在家里坐在电视前,观看和蔼可亲的主持人对某个产品的描述,同时还有一位模特将它展示出来。他们可以昼夜 24 小时购物,要买哪个商品,只需简单地打个电话,就可以用信用卡付款。家庭购物网深知热情顾客的影响力,还有名人顾客赞许该商品的魅力以及价格便宜的情感吸引力。

　　主要的时装设计师、大商场,甚至邮购公司也热衷于参加到家庭购物这一成功的活动中来。有些大百货公司正在尝试建立自己的电视频道,而一些零售商则计划在未来推出互动式电视购物。这样,电视观众就可以与他们自己个人的商店购物代理联系,询问产品情况并订购商品,而所有这一切都是通过他们的电视进行的。

　　电视购物能取代商场购物吗? 一些商业界人士宣称,家庭购物网代表着"未来的电子购物大商场"。然而对众多人来说,走出家门,在一家真正的商店购物乃是放松休闲的一种方式,甚至也是一种娱乐。还有,在许多购物者看来,摸一摸或试穿一下他们想买的商品,仍是重要的。正因如此,专家们说,将来在家购物会与商场购物并存,但决不会完全取代商场购物。

Exercises

Part 1　Reading Comprehension

Directions：*Decide whether the following statements are true or false according to the text. Write "T" for True and "F" for False.*

1~5　T　F　T　T　F·

2. Directions：*Read the passage carefully and complete the outline of the text.*

1) A.

　　a. relax; be entertained　b. touch

　　B.

　　a. fighting　　　　　　　b. in long lines　　　c. finding

2) A.

　　a. stay; sit　　　　　　b. describe; displayed　c. phone call; credit card

　　B.

　　a. touch　　　　　　　b. chance; enjoy

3）A. communication; interactively

   B. electronic shopping malls

   C. shopping

Part 2   Words & Structure

Directions：*Fill in each of the blanks with an appropriate word or phrase from the box. Change the form if necessary.*

1. networking
2. in line
3. around the clock
4. shopping
5. bargain
6. credit cards
7. go out
8. is experimenting with
9. alongside
10. place a... order

Part 3   Translation

Directions： *Translate the following sentences into English.*

1. I have long been tried of sitting in an office all day.
2. For customers, credit cards permit the purchase of goods and services even when funds are low.
3. If the words "charge it to the credit card" sound familiar, it is no wonder.
4. The debate will become even more heated if she joins in.
5. I am very eager to continue my education at your college.

Text B

参考译文

产品广告

广告是一种销售形式,靠直接的或人对人的销售是不实际的、不可能或效率低的销售方式。广告方式多种多样。人们可以通过报纸刊登简明扼要的通知或启事,也可以用杂志、广播、电视及直接邮购等方式做广告。

广告信息是通过各种媒体广泛传播的。当你打开收音机的时候,你会听到广告;当你看电视的时候,广告会跳入你的眼帘;如果你翻阅报纸杂志,又会看到广告;你走在大街上,鳞次栉比的广告牌会令你应接不暇。那些销售商整天挖空心思地吸引你的注意力,结果到处都是广告。

在西方,广告成为使大众媒体起作用的一种"造血工具"。许多电视台、报纸、杂志、广播电台都是私营的,政府不提供资金。钱从何而来呢? 从广告。没有广告,也就没有这些私营企业。

你是否问过自己什么是广告? 人们对这个问题持不同的答案。人们一度认为,广告是"使你在大众面前闻名退迹"的一种手段。而有些人认为广告是"用漂亮语言讲出来的事实"。现在,越来越多的人倾向用这种方法给它下定义:广告是由明确的发起人出资通过各种传播媒介达到劝说性展示产品、服务及理念的非个人的信息传播。

首先,广告通常是要付钱的,各种各样的赞助单位(人)要为我们从各种媒体看到的、读到的、听到的广告付钱。第二,做广告是非个人的,它通常不是面对面的交流。虽然,你可能感到某个广告传递的信息是针对你的,但事实上它是对群众的。第三,广告通常是劝说性的。直接或间接地催促人们购物。所有的广告都试图使人们深信广告中所宣传的产品、理念、服务都会使你受益。第四,出资做广告的赞助者的身份明确。我们可以从广告中看出赞助广告的是公司或者委员会,或者是个人。第五,做广告一般都通过传统和非传统大众媒体。传统媒体包括报纸、杂志、广播、电视、电影;非传统媒体包括邮件、火柴盒的封面和广告牌等。

Exercises

Part 1　Reading Comprehension

1. Directions: *Read the text carefully and discuss the following questions*

1) Advertising is used when direct, or person-to-person selling is impractical, impossible or inefficient.

2) Advertising techniques range from the publishing of simple, straight-forward notices in newspaper to the joint use of newspapers, magazines, television, radio, direct mail and so on.

3) In the West, advertisements are the fuel that makes mass media work. Many TV stations, newspapers, magazines, radio stations are privately owned. The government does not give them money. From advertisements, get the money they need to work. Without them, there would not be these private businesses.

4) Advertising is the paid, non-personal, and usually persuasive presentation of goods, services and ideas by identified sponsors through various media.

5) Various sponsors.

2. Directions: *Choose the best answer according to the text.*

1~5 A C A 　C B

Part 2　Words & Structure

Directions: *Fill in the blanks with the following words or phrases.*

1. inefficient　2. define　　3. competed　4. includes　　5. urged

6. techniques　7. convinced　8. benefited　9. identify　　10. aims at

Part 3　Translation

1. Directions: *Translate the following paragraph into Chinese.*

　　你是否问过自己什么是广告？人们对这个问题持不同的答案。人们一度认为,广告是"使你在大众面前闻名遐迩"的一种手段。而有些人认为广告是"用漂亮语言讲出来的事实"。现在,越来越多的人倾向用这种方法给它下定义:广告是由明确的发起人出资通过各种传播媒介达到劝说性展示产品、服务及理念的非个人的信息传播。

2. Directions: *Translate the following sentences into English by using the words or phrases given in the brackets.*

1) The students in our class range in age from 18 to 24.

2) Please turn on the radio.

3) The dress in the window caught her attention when she passed the store.

4) As a result he had been given an excellent job.

5) The two candidates will debate face to face.

6) Those girls' behavior is difficult to understand. What are they aiming at?

7) Will the AIDS patients benefit from the new drug?

8) I can't let you do it in this way.

Writing Practice

Directions: *Write a composition entitled "**Supermarkets**" with at least than 120 words (Not including the given opening sentence). Your composition* *should be based on the OUTLINE below and should start with the given opening sentence:* **"Since the first supermarket emerged fifty years ago, it has become the most popular shopping center in many large cities around the world."**

Sample

Supermarkets

Since the first supermarket emerged fifty years ago, it has become the most popular shopping center in many large cities around the world. In China, supermarkets enjoy an increasing popularity among city dwellers, especially the common people with low incomes.

Compared with other types of stores, supermarkets are getting popular for several reasons. First, fewer employees are required in supermarkets and management cost is reduced. Second, almost all goods are shipped directly from the producers and sold at considerably cheaper prices. Lastly, in supermarkets, almost every kind of daily necessity is available and placed on open shelves, so the customers can choose whatever they want from their shopping list and take the items to the checkout counter easily. As a result, instead of visiting many stores, customers can get the tiring shopping task done quickly and feel relaxed. What is more, many supermarkets stay open very late at night, and provide large parking spaces.

In the last few years, supermarkets have mushroomed in Beijing and many other large cities in China. The comfort and convenience of shopping in supermarkets please Chinese customers very much; and the supermarkets, steadily gaining popularity, are doing booming business in China.

(196 words)

Further Practice

Part 1 Multiple Choice

Directions: *There are 10 incomplete sentences in this part. For each sentence there* are four choices marked **A**, **B**, **C** and **D**. Choose the **ONE** that best completes the sentence.

1~5　A　D　D　A　B　　　　6~10　C　C　D　D　B

Part 2　Cloze

Directions： *There are 20 blanks in this passage, and for each blank there are four choices marked A, B, C, and D at the end of the passage. You should choose the **ONE** that best fits into the passage.*

1~5　C　A　B　C　B　　　　6~10　D　A　D　B　D
11~15　A　C　D　A　D　　　　16~20　B　C　A　B　C

Part 3　Reading Comprehension

Directions： *Read the following passage and then choose the best answer to the questions below it.*

1~4　D　C　D　D

Unit 6　　*Music*

Key & Difficult Points：(重点、难点)

New Words

due, precious, delicate, mostly, instrument, evolve, tradition, accompany, similar, spiritual, influence, popular, culture, amazing, attractive, tight, idol, career, perform, rarely, symbol, melody, autograph, caliber, competent, covet, faint, quaint, rapport

Phrases & Expressions

work on, work out, fall into place, feel like, start out, go back to, such as, come from, be similar to, have influence on/upon, not only... but also... , break up, take off

Exercises

Listening Practice：Section B (Exercise 1, 2)
Reading Practice：**Text A**　Part 2　Words & Structure (Exercise 1, 2)
　　　　　　　　　　　　　Part 3　Translation (Exercise 2)
　　　　　　　　　　Text B　Part 2　Words & Structure (Exercise1, 2)
　　　　　　　　　　　　　Part 3　Translation (Exercise 2)
Writing Practice
Further Practice：Part 1　Multiple Choice

Listening Practice

Section A

Key to

Exercise 1

Directions: *In this section, you will hear a song. Listen to the song carefully and fill in the blanks with the exact words you have just heard.*

(1) favorite   (2) smile   (3) lost   (4) shines

(5) fine   (6) cry   (7) rather   (8) changed

(9) memorize   (10) melt

Tape-script

Yesterday Once More

When I was young I'd listen to the radio waiting for my favorite songs.

When they played I'd sing along, it made me smile.

Those were such happy times and not so long ago,

How I wondered where they'd gone.

But they're back again just like a long lost friend

All the songs I love so well.

((A) Every shalalala, every wo-wo, still shines.

Every shingalingaling that they're starting to sing, so fine.)

When they get to the part, where he's breaking her heart,

It can really

((B) make me cry, just like before, it's yesterday once more.

Shoobie doobie do lang lang.)

Looking back on how it was in years gone by

And the good times that I had make today seem rather sad.

So much has changed.

It was songs of love that I would sing to them and I'd memorize each word,

Those old melodies still sound so good to me as they melt the years away.

(REPEAT A)

All my best memories come back clearly to me,

Some can even (REPEAT B.)

(REPEAT A TWICE AND FADE OUT.)

Section B

Key to

Exercise 1

Directions: *Listen to the dialogue and choose the best answer to complete each of the following statements.*

1~5   D   B   C   B   D

Exercise 2

Directions: *Listen to the dialogue again and write "T" (true) or "F"(false) for each statement you hear.*

1~5   F   F   T   T   F

Tape-script

Let's Go to the Movie

Wife: I'm tired of looking at television. Let's go to the movie tonight.

Husband: All right. Do you want to go downtown? Or is there a good movie in the neighborhood?

Wife: I'd rather not spend a lot of money. What does the paper say about neighborhood theaters?

Husband: Here's the list on page... Column 6. Here it is. Where's the Rialto? There's a good movie there.

Wife: That's too far away. And it's hard to find a place to park there.

Husband: Well, the Grand Theater has Gone with the Wind.

Wife: I saw that years ago. I don't want to see it again. Anyway, it's too long. We wouldn't get home until midnight.

Husband： The Center has a horror film. You wouldn't want to see that.

Wife： No, indeed. I wouldn't be able to sleep tonight.

Husband： That's about all there is. Unless we change our minds and go downtown.

Wife： No, we just can't afford it. There must be something else we haven't seen.

Husband： Here, look for yourself. I can't find anything else.

Wife： Look at this!

Husband： What?

Wife： In the television schedule, there's a baseball game on television tonight.

Husband： I wasn't looking for a TV program. I was looking at the movie ads.

Wife： I know, but I just happened to notice it. New York is playing Boston.

Husband： That ought to be good. I wouldn't mind watching that.

Wife： OK. Let's stay home. We can go to a movie Friday.

Oral Practice

参考译文

对话1

> **情景**
> 小张邀请他的好友小李加参周末音乐会。

小张:屋里有人吗?

小李:哈,是你呀! 今天是什么风把你给吹来了?

小张:想你嘛,难道你就不想我? 瞧瞧你的床铺和桌子乱七八糟,人看上去脸色苍白疲惫不堪。你究竟在忙什么?

小李:学期论文,下周三要交。我已经整整干了两天了,才搞了个提纲。真是苦不堪言。

小张:别紧张。如果你能放松一天,思路就自然畅通了。咱俩有一个多月没出去了。今晚有个音乐会,我搞了两张票,愿意和我一起去吗?

小李:太好了。演奏什么曲目?

小张:你没听说爱乐乐团在这儿吗?已经演出了两场西方古典音乐会了。今晚是最后一场了,机会难得。

小李:我想去,可我对西方音乐,尤其是古典音乐一窍不通。我恐怕理解不了。

小张:没关系。了解它的最好方法就是去听。

小李:这是真的。那么,我们什么时候出发?

小张:音乐会 8:00 开始。咱们最好 7:30 动身。我在宿舍等你。

小李:好吧。谢谢你的邀请。

对话 2

情景

　　小张和小李在音乐厅。演出当中他们小声谈论。

小张:哎呀,我们来得正是时候,音乐会还没开始呢。

小李:我们的座号是 10 排,18 号和 20 号。

小张:再稍微靠前点。

小李:到了,那边的两个位子。(对已经就座的听众说)劳驾。

小张:这是贝多芬的又一杰作。

小李:我读过有关贝多芬的故事,但是我从来没有听过他的乐曲。顺便问一句,他是你最喜欢的作曲家吗?

小张:是的,但不是惟一的。我也酷爱莫扎特、舒伯特、肖邦、舒曼、施特劳斯、柴可夫斯基及其他著名的作曲家。

小李:听,这支曲子棒极了。谁写的?

小张:施特劳斯的《蓝色的多瑙河》。这首曲子使我陶醉。《蓝色的多瑙河》被认为是"华尔兹之王"。每当我听到它就想翩翩起舞。

小李:你很会欣赏音乐。我要是有你那份音乐天赋就好了。

Reading Practice

Text A

参考译文

摇 滚 乐

很难说准确,我们所说的"摇滚乐"是如何起源的。它的根可以追溯到许多不同的国家、许多不同类型的音乐和音乐家。

摇滚乐主要由非洲的黑人音乐和欧洲的白人音乐发展而来。17世纪抵达美洲的欧洲人和黑奴各有其不同的音乐。非洲黑人惯用重击的鼓声、粗糙刺耳的歌喉、喊叫的曲调和齐声应答。欧洲白人主要是英格兰人和苏格兰人,则常用较强烈的旋律、不太重的鼓声以及诸如吉他、喇叭和提琴等乐器。摇滚乐的历史便是它从这两种传统音乐发展而来的历史。

从17世纪到20世纪,美国南部的音乐家们发展了两种音乐形式:通常由黑人演奏的"布鲁斯"(伤感的黑人民歌)和白人演奏的乡村音乐。黑人音乐家用吉他伴奏演唱"布鲁斯"。这种音乐类似劳动号子,叙述痛苦的故事,歌词常重复多次。"摇滚"一词可能来源于南方黑人的教堂,人们在那里唱着圣歌,并随着强烈的节奏舞蹈,这种节奏称为"摇摆和旋转"。同时,白人演奏乡村音乐,这种音乐大多是传统的舞曲和叙述悲伤故事的慢拍子歌曲。歌手们用弦乐器如提琴和吉他伴奏。

在此期间,"布鲁斯"音乐家与乡村音乐家之间相互有了一些影响。电吉他的诞生使(20世纪)40年代的乡村音乐和"布鲁斯"音乐发生了变化。电吉他的声音成了摇滚乐的声音。人们一想到早期的摇滚乐准会想到"摇滚乐之王"埃尔维斯·普莱斯利。这个背着吉他的青年改变了流行文化。埃尔维斯·普莱斯利是一个普通人,但是自从他在孟非斯录制了两首"布鲁斯"歌曲以后,一切都变了。他唱遍了南方各地,青少年们为他那惊人的嗓音和迷人的表演而疯狂。他演唱的音乐把白人的乡村音乐和黑人的"布鲁斯"音乐融为一体,非常激动人心。他留长发,穿紧身裤的形象成了青少年们的偶像。两年以后,他便风靡全国。

后来,埃尔维斯的事业便走向下坡。他的音乐缺少了他早期歌曲的生命力。然而,不仅在美国,而且在全世界,他仍然是摇滚乐的象征。他死于1977年,但他的音乐并未因他的死而消失。摇滚乐不断发展和变化,但摇滚乐的核心和灵魂仍然是埃尔维斯所表现的那个核心和灵魂。

Exercises

Part 1　Reading Comprehension

Directions:*Choose the best answer according to the text.*
1~5　C A D C A

Part 2　Words & Structure

1. Directions:*Match an expression in **Column B** which is similar in meaning to the **ONE** in **Column A**.*
1)~5)　j f h b d　　　6)~10)　i c a g e

2. Directions:*Fill in each of the blanks with an appropriate word from the box. Change the form if necessary.*

1）evolved　　　　　　　2）symbol

3）popular　　　　　　　4）similar

5）influence　　　　　　6）accompanies

7）amazing　　　　　　8）tight

9）tradition　　　　10）career

Part 3　Translation

1. Directions:*Translate the following passage into Chinese.*

　　音乐是我们生活中很重要的组成部分。音乐可以伴舞、伴饮、助餐，表达爱情和思想。有些歌曲能使我们想起童年和青年时代。还有一些歌曲会使我们想起我们所爱的人。许多重要场合，如婚礼和葬礼，都有专门的音乐。每一个国家都有自己的国歌，如美国的《星条旗》。在美国，中学和大学还有自己的校歌。

2. Directions:*Translate the following sentences into English.*

1）The dove is a symbol of peace.

2）The house is set in an attractive countryside.

3）He asked me to accompany him to the church.

4）The simple plan evolved into a complicated scheme.

5）This term may come from a French word.

Text B

参考译文

甲壳虫乐队

1980年当约翰·列农在他的纽约公寓外被他早期签过唱片封套的一个年轻男子杀死的时候,一个时代也宣告结束了。原先曾有人希望有一天甲壳虫乐队能重新组合到一起,现在这一丝希望破灭了,更重要的是,甲壳虫乐队所代表的乐观主义和他们传播的社会意识也烟消云散了。

1960年,乔治·哈里森、约翰·列农、保罗·麦卡特尼和林格·斯塔尔在利物浦创立了甲壳虫乐队。哈里森,列农和麦卡特尼以前曾在德国的汉堡有过俱乐部的演唱经验,但是甲壳虫乐队的真正的腾飞是在利物浦的卡文市,他们的故乡。

他们的第一张单曲《爱我吧》是在1962年10月发行的。四个月以后,他们的第二支单曲《给我快乐》飞快地进入排行榜的前十名,很快就占据了让人称羡的冠军位置,而他们第一张唱片也成了1963年最畅销的唱片。虽然他们的组合于1970年宣布解散,那时他们早已身价百万了。但是他们的唱片仍然行销全世界。是什么使甲壳虫乐队如此特殊?

作为一个组合,他们是有竞争力的,他们的声音很动听,但是这还不够。或许是人杰地灵使得他们幸运吧:生养他们的缤纷的默西赛德风光,他们对美国黑人节奏与布鲁斯音乐的喜爱;还有,他们彼此之间关系融洽,他们与歌迷的关系也很融洽,同时列农与麦特卡尼合写了一大批优秀的歌曲。

最初他们的题材总是那些年青歌迷感兴趣和关心的:爱情,忧伤,好运,厄运,以及任何大城市都有的怪人。后来,他们开始反映20世纪60年代的气候,唱社会的不平等和政治的不公平。此外,他们创作的歌曲旋律丰富,有创新意味,足可以被卓越的音乐大师巴锡和埃拉·菲茨杰拉德演唱并演奏。

甲壳虫乐队很特别,因为他们相信自己的才华。他们不抄袭任何人,他们也足够坚强,因为他们不让难以想象的突然成功毁灭了他们。在这方面,他们可能应该感谢他们的唱片制作人乔治·马丁和他们的经理布莱恩·爱泼斯坦。甲壳虫乐队的特殊之处还因为在那个社会和政治理想大幻灭的时代,他们是一股乐观的力量。他们是当时年轻人的声音。

Exercises

Part 1 Reading Comprehension

Directions：*Please answer each of the following questions with no more than 10 words.*

1. Singer and fan.
2. Optimism and social consciousness.
3. In 1960，in Liverpool.
4. In February，1963.
5. In 1970.

Part 2 Words & Structure

1. Directions：*Match an expression in* **Column B** *which is similar in meaning to the* **ONE** *in* **Column A**.

1)~5) b d i h c   6)~10) g a j e f

2. Directions：*Fill in each of the blanks with an appropriate word from the box. Change the form if necessary.*

1）competent   2）faintest
3）melody   4）formed
5）covet   6）quaint
7）rapport

Part 3 Translation

1. Directions：*Translate the following passage into Chinese.*

　　在很多方面我们可以说约翰·贝尔茨是世界上最成功的作曲家。他写的每一支歌都保证可以成为一支真正的好歌——不是在流行音乐排行榜上，而是在孩子们的心中。原因是因为贝尔茨写的每一支歌都是为了一个得重病的孩子。他的歌从来都能成功地使孩子微笑，使他们振作。他们也一遍一遍地放这些歌。这对于贝尔茨来说比高居排行榜要有意义得多。

2. Directions：*Translate the following sentences into English.*

1）The boys coveted his new hat.

2）I like that song; it has a pleasant melody.

3）He is a statesman of the highest caliber.

4）He is competent for the task.

5）The sounds fainted away in the distance.

Writing Practice

Directions: *This part is to test your ability to do practical writing. You are required to write **an invitation letter**, You can write it according to the instructions given in Chinese.*

写作指导：

邀请信分正式和非正式两种。正式邀请用请柬，通常是印好的，有一定的格式。但在习惯上邀请者和被邀请者都用第三人称。写请柬时必须将内容、时间说清楚。被邀请者收到请柬后，不管接受与否都应回复。请柬中的姓名要拼写完整，时间要用文字表示，不用阿拉伯数字。同时还要表达希望对方接受邀请的诚挚愿望。

基本句型：

1. I would like to know if you could... 不知您能否前来……

2. I would like to invite you to... 我请您……

3. I would like to take this opportunity to invite you to... 借此机会，我想邀请您……

4. Please let us know as soon as possible if you can come and tell us when you can make the trip. 请您尽早与我们联系，并告知能否出行及具体的时间。

5. Please accept our warm welcome and sincere invitation. 请接受我们热情的欢迎和诚挚的邀请。

Sample

December 2，2006.

Dear Mr. & Mrs. Smith,

How are you going?

Haven't seen you for a long time. I just heard that you have come back from hometown. You know, we miss you very much. How about coming to have

68

dinner with us at 6:30 at our house on the afternoon of December 8, 2006? We do hope you would join us. After dinner, let's go to enjoy the concert.

It's really a pleasure to spend a day with you.

Yours sincerely,
Mr. & Mrs. Wang Hua

(89 words)

Further Practice

Part 1　Multiple Choice

Directions: *There are 10 incomplete sentences in this part. For each sentence there are four choices marked **A**, **B**, **C** and **D**. Choose the **ONE** that best completes the sentence.*

1~5　A　B　B　D　A　　　6~10　C　B　D　B　B

Part 2　Cloze

Directions: *Fill in the blanks with the proper words.*

(1) is　　　(2) into　　　(3) first　　　(4) to　　　(5) in

(6) such as　(7) music　　(8) from　　(9) popular　(10) used

Part 3　Reading Comprehension

Directions: *Choose the best answer after reading the following passage.*

1~5　B　A　D　A　C

Unit 7 *Travel*

Key & Difficult Points：(重点、难点)

New Words

fair, cancellation, vacant, track, solo, determined, voyage, previously, attempt, dissuade, treacherous, contact, accomplish, experience, conquer, conference, delighted, form, eventually, destination, lounge, sleepy, imagine

Phrases & Expressions

get off, information desk, token booth, slip into, all by oneself, set off, in spite of, by far, turn over, can not help, sink into, fall asleep

Exercises

Listening Practice：Section B(Exercise 1, 2)
Reading Practice：**Text A**　Part 2　Words & Structure (Exercise 1, 2)
　　　　　　　　　　　Part 3　Translation (Exercise 2)
　　　　　　　　Text B　Part 2　Words & Structure (Exercise 1, 2)
　　　　　　　　　　　Part 3　Translation (Exercise 2)
Writing Practice
Further Practice：Part 1　Multiple Choice
　　　　　　　　　Part 2　Cloze

Listening Practice

Key to

Exercise 1

Directions: *In this section, you will hear a song. Listen to the song carefully and fill in the blanks with the exact words you have just heard.*

(1) sailing	(2) Home	(3) stormy	(4) flying
(5) sky	(6) high	(7) with	(8) hear
(9) Through	(10) far	(11) dying	(12) Lord

Tape-script

Sailing

Rod Stewart

I am sailing, I am sailing,
Home again, across the sea.
I am sailing stormy waters,
To be near you, to be free.
I am flying, I am flying,
Like a bird, across the sky.
I am flying passing high clouds,
To be with you, to be free.
Can you hear me? Can you hear me?
Through the dark night far away.
I am dying, forever crying,
To be with you; who can say?
Can you hear me? Can you hear me?
Through the dark night far away.
I am dying, forever crying,
To be with you; who can say?

We are sailing, we are sailing,
Home again across the sea.
We are sailing stormy waters,
To be near you, to be free.
Oh, Lord, to be near you, to be free.
Oh, Lord, to be near you, to be free.
Oh, Lord, to be near you, to be free.
Oh, Lord.

Section B

Key to

Exercise 1

Directions: *Listen to the dialogue and choose the best answer to complete each of the following statements.*

1~5　C　D　C　D　B

Exercise 2

Directions: *Listen to the dialogue again and write "T" (true) or "F" (false) for each statement you hear.*

1~6　T　F　F　T　T

Tape-script

Tokyo — a City Rebuilt

Tokyo, the capital of Japan, is one of the largest cities in the world. It is also one of the world's most modern cities. Twice this century, the city was destroyed and rebuilt. In 1923 a major earthquake struck the city. Thousands of people were killed and millions were left homeless as buildings collapsed and fires broke out throughout Tokyo. It took seven years to rebuild the city. During World War II, Tokyo was destroyed once again. As a result of these disasters there is nothing of old Tokyo remaining in the downtown area.

After the war, the people of Tokyo began to rebuild their city. Buildings went up at a fantastic rate, and between 1945 and 1960, the city's population more than doubled. Because of the Olympic Games held in Tokyo in 1964, many new stadiums, parks and hotels were built to accommodate visitors from all over the world. As a result of this rapid development, however, many problems have arisen. Housing shortage, pollution, and waste disposal have presented serious challenges to the city, but the government has begun several programs to answer them.

Oral Practice

参考译文

对话1

情景

方玲是一个中国留学生,她想去唐人街。此刻,她在纽约地铁站。

方玲:	太好了,问讯处就在那里。请问到唐人街哪一站下?
车站职员:	你到运河街下车。
方玲:	我该坐快车还是慢车?
车站职员:	坐快车吧。这可以节省你许多时间。慢车每站都停。
方玲:	要多少钱?
车站职员:	一元五角。你在买币处换成专用辅币。
方玲:	我怎样用这辅币?
车站职员:	你在入口处转门那儿把辅币塞进投币孔里,就能推动转门进去了。
方玲:	你能告诉我去站台怎么走吗?
车站职员:	走到那里过6号检票口,火车马上就要来了。
方玲:	一个人搭地铁很危险吗?
车站职员:	我知道晚上确实很危险,但白天很安全。

对话 2

情景

方玲现在在纽约火车站售票口,准备去华盛顿。

方玲:　到华盛顿车票多少钱?

售票员:　40 美元。

方玲:　下一班列车什么时间发车?

售票员:　有一列车 10:30 发,另一列下午 2:40 发。

方玲:　都是直达车吗?

售票员:　10:30 那列车是快车,另一列是慢车。

方玲:　两列车上都有餐车吗?

售票员:　10:30 那列有餐饮供应,2:40 的只有一个休息车厢,供应三明治、咖啡、饮料等。

方玲:　你能帮我看一下还有没有卧铺票吗? 多少钱一张?

售票员:　卧铺票 80 美元。10:30 那列有一节卧铺车厢,不过,今天这趟车的卧铺票没有了。但临开车前也许有退票。火车离站前总能问清。

方玲:　今晚的车有带卧铺车厢的吗?

售票员:　有一趟卧铺车你可以坐,11:50 离站。刚刚有人退了票,所以我这儿有两个空位。

方玲:　我要了。请问这趟车停靠几号轨道?

售票员:　5 号轨道。

方玲:　谢谢。

售票员:　不客气。

Reading Practice

Text A

参考译文

环球航行

弗朗西斯·奇切斯特在独自驾船作环球航行之前,他曾试图作环球飞行,但没有成功。那是在 1931 年。

　　好多年过去了。他放弃了飞行，开始航海。他领略到航海的巨大乐趣。奇切斯特在首届横渡大西洋单人航海比赛中夺魁时，已经 58 岁。他周游世界的宿愿重又被唤起，奇切斯特决意实施自己的计划，不过这一次他是要驾船环游。1966 年 8 月，在他快年满 65 岁的时候，他开始了一生中最了不起的一次航海。不久，他就驾着那艘 16 米长的新船吉普赛·莫思号启程出海了。

　　奇切斯特沿着 19 世纪大型三桅帆船的航线航行。不过，三桅帆船拥有众多船员，而奇切斯特却是独个儿扬帆破浪。奇切斯特一直航行了 14,100 英里，到了澳大利亚的悉尼港才停船靠岸。这段航程比以往单人驾舟航海的最远航程还多一倍多。他于 12 月 12 日抵达澳大利亚，这一天正是他离开英国的第 107 天。奇切斯特上岸后，得由人搀扶着才能行走。

　　在悉尼休息了几周之后，他不顾朋友们的多方劝阻，再次扬帆出航。这后半段航程更艰险，在此期间，他绕过了险情四伏的合恩角。

　　1 月 29 日他驶离澳大利亚。第二天夜晚——这是他所经历过的最黑暗的一个夜晚，海面上波涛汹涌，小船几乎被风浪掀翻。幸好小船遭到的损坏还不算太严重。奇切斯特镇静地钻进被窝，睡着了。等他醒来时，大海又恢复了平静。然而，他仍禁不住想到，要是果真有什么意外，他能借无线电联系上的人，最近的也要在 885 英里以外的岛上，除非附近哪儿有条轮船。

　　1967 年 5 月 28 日，星期天，晚上将近九点，他回到了英国。伊丽莎白女王二世手持宝剑赐封他为爵士，将近 400 年前，伊丽莎白一世也曾手持同一把宝剑，把爵位赐予完成首次环球航行的弗朗西斯·德雷克爵士。从英国出发，再回到英国，整个航程长达 28,500 英里。奇切斯特一共花了九个月的时间，其中实际航行时间为 226 天。他终于完成了他想完成的伟业。

　　像许多别的冒险家一样，奇切斯特产生过恐惧而又战胜了恐惧。在这一过程中，他无疑对自身有了一些了解。此外，在当今这个人类如此依赖机器的时代，他赋予了全世界的人们以新的自豪感。

Exercises

Part 1　Reading Comprehension

Directions：*Answer the following questions according to the text.*

1. He was nearly sixty-five years old.
2. Gipsy Moth and 16-meter long.
3. He followed the route of the great nineteenth century clipper ships.

4. 14, 100 miles.

5. His friends tried to dissuade him from continuing his sailing.

Part 2　Words & Structure

1. Directions:*Match an expression in **Column B** which is similar in meaning to the **ONE** in **Column A**.*

1)～5)　e　g　f　b　h　　　6)～10)　a　c　j　d　i

2. Directions:*Fill in each of the blanks with an appropriate word or phrase from the box. Change the form if necessary.*

1) contact

2) conquered

3) experienced

4) all by herself

5) attempt

6) accomplished

7) by far

8) was determined

9) previously

10) set off

Part 3　Translation

1. Directions:*Translate the following passage into Chinese.*

　　在美国大部分城市里,如果你去的地方不远,最快的方法是步行。在上班时间(周一到周五上午9点到下午5点),大多数街道交通拥挤,有时甚至出现塞车停顿的状况。所以很多人宁愿走路。

2. Directions:*Translate the following sentences into English.*

1) Mother told us that Mount Huang was the highest mountain she had ever climbed。

2) He is determined to continue his experiment but this time he'll do it another way.

3) When she read the novel，she couldn't help thinking of the five years she had spent in the countryside.

4) He was born in this very room 20 years ago.

5) You cannot make great progress in English without good study habits.

76

Text B

参考译文

一次旅行经历

当吉姆·布鲁斯应邀参加计算机网络的国际会议时，他很高兴。会议将在日内瓦举行。吉姆心想这是带玛丽度假的好机会。他们决定先去巴黎待一星期，然后吉姆去日内瓦开会，玛丽回家。

吉姆和玛丽在巴黎待了一星期，玩得非常开心。他们走了很多路，周末他们都感到很疲倦。吉姆陪玛丽来到机场，送她上了飞往伦敦的班机。就在他在候机大厅等待飞往日内瓦的班机时，天起雾了。他的飞机终于在两小时后起飞，吉姆一头扎到座位上睡着了。

不巧的是，飞机快要到日内瓦时，雾更浓了，变成了大雾。飞行员和目的地联络上后，被告知由于雾大不能着陆。在把这个消息通知给旅客时，吉姆还在熟睡。等飞机返回巴黎着陆时他才醒。他迷迷糊糊地急忙走出大厅，叫了一辆出租车。他让司机送他到日内瓦国际酒店。惊讶的司机看着他，好像他发疯了。他问吉姆是否真要出租车，吉姆说"是的"，因为他太累了，走不动了。这时司机大笑起来，说走250英里去日内瓦简直无法想象。听到这话，吉姆完全清醒了。他问司机这是什么地方，司机告诉他是在巴黎，如果想去日内瓦最好坐飞机。司机说，雾已经开始消散了。这时吉姆的头脑也开始清醒了。

Exercises

Part 1 Reading Comprehension

Directions：*Choose the best answer according to the text.*
·1~6 A A D C B C

Part 2 Words & Structure

1. Directions：*Match an expression in* **Column B**，*which is similar in meaning to the ONE in* **Column A**.
1)~5) i e c f h   6)~10) g b a j d

2. Directions：*Fill in each of the blanks with an appropriate word or phrase* *from the box. Change the form if necessary.*

1) conference   2) delighted

3) imagine   4) sank into

5) took off   6) destination

7) had better   8) woke up

9) take place   10) asleep

Part 3   Translation

1. Directions: *Translate the following passage into Chinese.*

城市里用得最多的交通工具是公交车。在很多城市里乘客要自备零钱,也就是说上车时你的车费得不多不少正好。在很多地方你可以买辅币,就是当钱用的小硬币,在城市各个角落都可以买到。

2. Directions: *Translate the following sentences into English.*

1) Mary simply can't imagine a life without TV.

2) Shanghai is not my destination. I just change the train there.

3) The plane is taking off in an hour. We'd better hurry up.

4) It's nine o'clock. It's impossible to catch the plane.

5) He can't come this afternoon because he has to attend a conference.

6) The children had fallen asleep when I got home.

Writing Practice

Directions: *This part is to test your ability to do practical writing. You are required to fill in the Registration Form according to the information given below. You can do it according to the instructions given in Chinese.*

写作指导:

住宿登记表常包含以下内容:姓名、性别、出生日期、国籍、身份、职业、停留原因、期限。有时还要求填写抵达日期、何处来何处去、房间号码、房间种类、房价、结账时间及付款方式等。如果是由代理人代办,还要注明代理人姓名、代理机构名称及代理人或机构的联系方式。填写住宿登记表时,语言要简洁,信息要真实,重点要突出,并避免出现误差。

常用语：

1. check in time/check out time 入住时间/结账时间
2. room type 房间种类
3. room rate 房价
4. means of payment 付款方式
5. in cash/by check/by credit card 现金/支票/信用卡
6. Single room/double room/twin room 单人房/双人房/双人房
7. suite(president suite，executive suite，mini suite)套房(总统套房,经理套房,小套房)
8. meeting room/multi-purpose hall/fitness center 会议室/多功能厅/健身中心
9. single bed/double bed/king size bed 单人床/双人床/大号床

Sample

Registration Form of Temporary Residence for Foreigners

Name in full	Sex
Tom Smith	Male
Date of birth	
May. 23,1972	
Nationality	Identity or occupation
U. S. A	Tourist
Visa or travel document number and date of validity(omitted)	
Object of stay	Date of arrivalll
Sighteeing	April,28,2006
Where from and to	Duration of stay
From Japan，to France	A week
Room number 1101	RMB 400

外国人临时住宿登记表

姓名	性别
汤姆 史密斯	男
出生日期	
1972 年 5 月 23 日	
国籍	来华身份或职业
美国	旅游

(续表)

签证或旅行证号码及期限(略)

停留事由	抵达日期
观光	2006 年 4 月 28 日
何处来何处去	拟住时间
从日本来,到法国去	一星期
房号或住址	房价
第 1101 号房间	RMB 400

Further Practice

Part 1　Multiple Choice

Directions：*There are 10 incomplete sentences in this part. For each sentence there are four choices marked **A**, **B**, **C** and **D**. Choose the **ONE** that best completes the sentence.*

1~5　C　D　D　D　A　　　　6~10　B　A　B　C　B

Part 2　Cloze

Directions：*Fill in the blanks with the proper words.*

(1) from
(2) down
(3) way
(4) plane
(5) Between
(6) give
(7) hot
(8) out
(9) ground
(10) until

Part 3　Reading Comprehension

Directions：*Choose the best answer after reading the following passage.*

1~5　A　A　C　D　C

Unit 8 ★ *Holidays*

Key & Difficult Points: (重点、难点)

New Words

potato, wine, actually, scent, mature, perfume, celebrate, practice, ancient, evil, attend, joyful, scene, occur, supply, fruit, refuse, enthusiastically, participate, parade, creative

Phrases & Expressions

plenty of, come by, look for, plan to do, get together, be popular with, base on, at the end of, stay up, pay calls on, dress up, participate in, too...to

Exercises

Listening Practice: Section B(Exercises 1, 2)
Reading Practice: **Text A**   Part 2   Words & Structure (Exercise)
                                      Part 3   Translation (Exercise)
                        Text B   Part 2   Words & Structure (Exercise)
                                      Part 3   Translation (Exercise)
Writing Practice
Further Practice: Part 1   Multiple Choice
                        Part 2   Cloze

Listening Practice

Section A

Key to

Exercise

Directions: *In this section, you will hear a song. Listen to the song carefully and*
fill in the blanks with the exact words you have just heard.

(1) way	(2) sleigh	(3) way	(4) sleigh
(5) snow	(6) sleigh	(7) fields	(8) laughing
(9) ring	(10) bright	(11) sing	(12) tonight

Tape-script

Jingle Bells

Jingle bells, jingle bells, jingle all the way.
Oh! What fun it is to ride in a one-horse open sleigh.
Jingle bells, jingle bells, jingle all the way.
Oh! What fun it is to ride in a one-horse open sleigh.
Dashing through the snow in a one-horse open sleigh.
Over the fields we go, laughing all the way.
Bells on bobtail ring, making spirits bright.
What fun it is to ride and sing a sleighing song tonight.

Section B

Key to

Exercise 1

Directions: *Listen to the following passage and choose the best answer.*
1~4 A B B C

Tape-script

Saint Valentine's Day

Several different stories are told about the origin of Saint Valentine's Day. One legend dates as far back as the days of the Roman Empire. According to the story, Claudius, the Emperor of Rome, wanted to increase the size of his army. He knew that it would be easier to get young men who were not married to join. Therefore he made a rule that no young man could marry until he had served a certain number of years in the army.

A priest named Valentine broke the rule and secretly married a great many young people. Finally, Claudius found out about Valentine and put the priest in prison, where he remained until his death on February 14.

After his death, Valentine was made a saint, and the day of his death was named Saint Valentine's Day. It became the custom for lovers to send each other messages on this day. Now saint Valentine's Day is a time for people to give roses and to send greetings.

Exercise 2

Directions: *Listen to the following passage and choose the best answer.*
1~5　C　A　D　B　C

Tape-script

The students at a certain American University used to play jokes on each other. When one of them had a girl-friend to visit him for the first time, the others would take all the furniture out of the students' room so when she arrived, there would be nothing to sit on.

Jack was a country boy who had never left his birth-place until he entered that university. When he heard about this joke, he disliked it and said to the other students, "I won't let this happen to me. I'm going to lock my door."

When Jack brought his girl-friend to his room for the first time, he was surprised to find that all the furniture was there — but the door was gone.

Oral Practice

参考译文

对话1

情景

王南来自中国，现正在美国留学。他的同学苏是美国人。她打算在家里举办感恩节派对。王南第一次在美国过感恩节。现在他们在教室里谈话。

苏： 嗨，王南。感恩节你有什么打算吗？

王南： 我没什么打算。

苏： 很好。今晚我要在家里要举办个聚会。你来吗？

王南： 当然，我非常乐意。我应该带什么东西吗？

苏： 不用了。到时候会有丰盛的沙拉、火腿、玉米、马铃薯、酒，当然还有火鸡。

王南： 听起来真棒。要我早一点来帮忙吗？

苏： 不用了。晚上七点左右来就行了。

王南： 那就晚上见吧。再见。

苏： 再见。

对话2

情景

圣诞节将至，布朗先生来到一家商店，他打算给母亲买件礼物。但是他又不确定买什么。一名售货员给了他一些建议。下面是他们的对话：

S：先生，您好！请问有什么要帮助的吗？

B：哦，是的。我正在给我母亲挑选圣诞礼物，但不知道选什么……

S：明白了，哎，这种香水怎么样？它的名字叫作"天堂味道"，很受成熟女性的欢迎呢。

B：真的不知道，我对香水从来都拿不定主意。

S：是的，可能很困难，是吧？那么，现在您可以考虑给她买这种高级唇膏。它有很多漂亮的颜色……

B：好，那我就买唇膏吧，你认为哪种颜色适合我母亲呢？她快60岁了。

S：这样的话我认为深红色会比较好一些。

B：好的，就拿支深红色的吧。

Reading Practice

Text A

参考译文

欢迎新年

世界上每个国家都庆祝新年，但庆祝的日期未必都一样。美洲和欧洲的人们都在一月一日庆祝新年。这一活动是从罗马人那里传下来的。罗马统治者恺撒把新年的日期从三月一号改到了一月一号。在中东，新年是春天开始的时候。中国人在春节时候庆祝新年，这一天也是阴历的第一天。春节往往在1月21日和2月19日之间，而犹太人的岁首节则在夏末的时候。

所有的文化习俗中有一项是共用的就是制造响声。古时候人们弄出响声来驱除家里的鬼神，如今很多人都放鞭炮。在日本，人们走家串户用鼓和竹棍来制造响声，而丹麦的年轻人往朋友房子的墙壁上扔瓶子或罐子的碎片。

在美国，很多人除夕夜守夜，看着时钟从这一年指到下一年。朋友们除夕夜欢聚在一起，当新年到来的时候，所有的钟都敲响，号角也吹响，大家互相亲吻对方。

许多欧洲国家里，一家人多到教堂去做礼拜来迎接新年，接下来朋友和亲戚间互相拜访一下。意大利的孩子们通常在新年的那天还能得到红包。

在法国和苏格兰，新年比圣诞节更加喜庆。在这些国家圣诞节仅仅是个宗教节日，而新年才是大家赠送礼物、聚会和拜访的时候。

Exercises

Part 1　Reading Comprehension

Directions: *Decide whether the following statements are True or false according to the text. Write "**T**" for true and write "**F**" for False.*

1~5　F　F　F　F　T　　　　6~7　T　F

Part 2　Words & Structure

Directions：*There are 10 incomplete sentences in this part. For each sentence there are four choices marked A, B, C and D. Choose the **ONE** that best completes the sentence.*

1~5　C　A　D　A　D　　　　6~10　B　A　C　B　B

Part 3　Translation

Directions：*Translate the following sentences into English.*

1. At the end of the letter, she sent her regards to my family.

2. Last night Bob stayed up late to watch the football game.

3. My parents moved from their hometown to this city 20 years ago.

4. After the match, the team members held a party to celebrate their victory.

5. Eating dumplings on Spring Festival is a practice in China.

Text B

参考译文

万圣节一幕

在节日期间你有没有见过鬼魂呢? 如果没有的话,就到这里看看吧。

一个冷冷的秋天的夜里。布朗夫人正坐在她的起居室里看书。突然门外传来很大的敲门声,紧接着又有几声。布朗夫人挂好门上的安全链,把门拉开一条缝往外看。门外站着三个孩子,带着面具穿着服装。一看见她,他们喊道:"要花招还是给招待! 给钱还是给吃的!"

布朗夫人往每个孩子的袋子里各装了一大块糖,然后对一个戴着大大的帽子、穿着高筒靴、用皮套别着一把玩具枪的小孩说:"你是干什么的?""牛仔",小孩答道。"我是鬼",另一个拿白床单裹住身子的小孩说道。"我是骷髅",第三个小孩说,"我的骨头会在暗处发光"。这个"骷髅"穿着黑色的衣服,上面画着白色的骨头。"谢谢您的糖块",孩子们边喊边跑着去按别人家的门铃。"欢迎你们来",布朗夫人说,"玩得高兴点啊,别再搞恶作剧了"。

每年 10 月 31 号,像这样的万圣节景象在美国到处可见。孩子们喜欢用服装打扮自己,做"花招还是招待"游戏。如果大人不给招待的话,比如糖块、饼干、水果或钱等,孩子们就会搞个恶作剧。比较典型的恶作剧有:在窗户上涂上肥皂水,用蜡笔在门上作画,把垃圾筒弄翻,把钉子塞进门铃里让它响个不停,往车上或朋友身上喷剃须膏等。

尽管万圣节是孩子们最热衷的节日,大人们有时也会有所行动。大学生和一些成年人会参加化妆舞会或是万圣节游行。商业区也经常用南瓜灯、稻草人和巫婆来装扮。有时平时看起来很严肃、辛勤工作的成年人也会在上班的时候装扮成一管牙膏或是垃圾筒。有时通过一些新奇的着装让朋友们感到吃惊,每个人都不会因为年纪的缘故而享受不到由此带来的乐趣。

Exercises

Part 1 Reading Comprehension

Directions:*Choose the best answer according to the text.*
1~5 C D B A C

Part 2 Words & Structure

Directions:*There are 10 incomplete sentences in this part. For each sentence there are four choices marked **A**, **B**, **C** and **D**. Choose the **ONE** that best completes the sentence.*
1~5 D A B C D   6~10 A B A D B

Part 3 Translation

Directions:*Translate the following sentences into Chinese.*
1. 每年 10 月 31 号,像这样的万圣节景象在美国到处可见。
2. 这个"骷髅"穿着黑色的衣服,上面画着白色的骨头。
3. 有时平时看起来很严肃、辛勤工作的成年人也会在上班的时候装扮成一管牙膏或是垃圾筒。
4. 尽管万圣节是孩子们最热衷的节日,大人们有时也会有所行动。
5. 每个人都不会因为年纪的缘故而享受不到由此带来的乐趣。

Writing Practice

Directions: *Write a composition on the topic: "The Lunar New Year". You should write at least 120 words according to the suggestions given below in Chinese.*

Sample

The Lunar New Year

The Lunar New Year is a great occasion to the Chinese people. It lasts about the first four days of the year, during which people do not work except for the workers on duty. Students do not go to school, and shops are closed. Several days before the New Year, people begin to prepare. Farmers kill pigs, sheep, cocks and hens. City dwellers buy meat, fish and vegetables. Houses are cleaned, couplets are pasted on the doors. Colorful lanterns are hung at the gates.

On the eve of the New Year, each family has its members gathered together and eats a family reunion dinner. After the meal they watch TV until the clock strikes twelve. Then every family sets off long strings of small firecrackers and other fireworks to welcome the New Year.

On the first day of the New Year, almost everyone is dressed in his or her best. When people meet on the way, they say to each other "Happy New Year". Friends and relatives pay new year calls and give presents to each other. Children indulge themselves in games.

(182 words)

Further Practice

Part 1   Multiple Choice

Directions: *There are 10 incomplete sentences in this part. For each sentence there are four choices marked **A**, **B**, **C** and **D**. Choose the **ONE** that best* *completes the sentence.*

1~5 C B D C B   6~10 D A C B A

Part 2   Cloze

Directions: *There are 10 blanks in the following passage. For each blank there are four choices marked A, B, C and D. Choose the ONE that best fits into the passage.*

1~5 D C A C B   6~10 D A C C B

Part 3   Reading Comprehension

Directions: *Choose the best answer after reading the following passage.*

1~5 B D C D C

Unit 9 *Business*

Key & Difficult Points：(重点、难点)

New Words

previous，manufacture，catalogue，remarkable，professional，complex，self-sufficient，utilize，scatter，consume，internally，innovation，beneficial，compel，available，conserve，ownership，stockholder，fraction，reverse，optimist，pessimist，notion，origin，myth，mnemonic，derive

Phrases & Expressions

be available，place restrictions on，be subjected to，channel into，board of directors，vice versa，come to be/do...，neither 和 nor 之后接同一词类的词，或同一词类的短语，"neither...nor..."为主语时，谓语动词须与 nor 之后的名词一致，the...the...的用法。

Exercises

Listening Practice：Section A
Reading Practice：**Text A** Part 2 Words & Structure（Exercise）
　　　　　　　　　　Part 3 Translation（Exercise 2）
　　　　　　　Text B Part 2 Words & Structure（Exercise）
　　　　　　　　　　Part 3 Translation（Exercise 2）
Writing Practice
Further Practice：Part 1 Multiple Choice

Listening Practice

Section A

Key to

Exercise

Directions: *Listen to the passage once and decide whether the following statements are true or false. Write "**T**" for True and "**F**" for False.*

1~5　F　T　F　F　T

Tape-script

Mr. , Mrs. , Miss. , and Ms.

Almost everyone knows the meanings of Mr. , Mrs. , and Miss. Mr. is used before the names of men. Mrs. is for married women and Miss. is for single women. But what is Ms. ?

For some time, businessmen in the United States have used Ms. before a woman's name when they do not know whether the woman is married or not. Today, however, many women prefer to use Ms. rather than Mrs. or Miss. The word Mr. does not tell us whether or not a man is married. Many women think this is an advantage for men. They want to be equal to men in this way. These women feel that it isn't important for people to know whether they are married or not.

There are some problems with Ms. , however. Not all women like it. Some like the older ways of doing things. Some find it difficult to pronounce. (Ms. sounds like "miz".) Generally, young women like it better than older women do. It is difficult to know whether or not Ms. will be used by more American women in the future. What do you think of this change?

Section B

Key to

Exercise

Directions: *You will hear 5 short conversations. After you hear a conversation and the question about it, read the four possible answers in your book and choose the best one to the question you have heard.*

1~5   A   B   D   D   C

Tape-script

1. Man: I understand that there is to be a showing of a new French film at the campus cinema. Would you like to come with me?

   Woman: I'd love to, but I'm afraid I can't understand the language.

   Third Voice: What language is spoken in the film?

2. Man: For the fourth year in a row the German team has won the bobsled race at the Winter Olympic.

   Woman: Good for them. But I really can't get excited about the sport.

   Third Voice: How many times before had the German team won the bobsled race?

3. Man: I've just picked up this book at the library. Have you ever read it?

   Woman: No. I rarely get a chance to read these days. I watch too much television.

   Third Voice: Where had the man just been?

4. Man: I can come to your house and pick you up in half an hour. Is that all right?

   Woman: Good. That means you'll be there at eight thirty.

   Third Voice: What time is it now?

5. Woman: Julia seems to be a very shy type of person.

   Man: Actually, she's not. She acts that way only with strangers.

   Third Voice: How well does the woman appear to know Julia?

Oral Practice

Establishing Business Relations

参考译文

对话 1

情景

　　一家中国医药公司想要拓展海外市场。小王是这家公司的销售员，他正在拜访一位美国外贸官员怀特先生。

小王：您是怀特局长吗？我姓王。李先生介绍我来见您。

怀特：噢，您是王先生。很高兴认识您。李先生是美国的老朋友。您以前和我们有来往吗？

小王：还没有呢。我们公司生产中药，相信会很适合美国人民的需要。我们希望出口到美国去。

怀特：我看这样吧，您写一封信，附上贵公司的产品目录，寄到我们纽约外贸局去。我们就可以安排您到纽约去洽谈。

对话 2

情景

　　许先生是一家中国电子产品公司的营销部经理。在国际博览会上，他正与一位新客户、ABC贸易公司的乔治·布朗先生谈话。

布朗：请问，你能告诉我什么地方有电子产品吗？

许：　这个区有。我们很高兴领您去看您需要的东西。这是我的名片。

布朗：谢谢。您是……

许：　我姓许。

布朗：很抱歉，我的拼音不好。这是我的名片。我是ABC贸易公司的乔治·布朗。我们进口电子产品和晶体管产品。

许： 请看看我们的样品。

布朗：你们的电子产品发展显著。

许： 是的，我们的研究有了好的结果了。

布朗：你们生产数码摄像机吗？

许： 是的。我们生产四种型号不同用途的数码摄像机。

布朗：有没有用来水下摄像的？

许： 有。这种型号是用来在水下摄像的，很专业。

布朗：我知道了。我想我已经发现了一些我们可能订购的产品，尽管我可能对它们还要进一步研究。

许： 好，非常欢迎。

布朗：我可能明天告诉您。

许： 那我明天上午等您，九点钟吧。

布朗：好，明天上午九点。到时见。

Reading Practice

Text A

参考译文

为什么要进出口

在当今复杂的经济社会里，不论是个人还是国家都不是自给自足的。不同的国家使用不同的经济资源；不同的人拥有不同的技能，这就是国际贸易及经济活动的基础。

国际贸易即国家之间的货物与商品交换，其产生有很多原因。首先，没有一个国家拥有其所需的一切商品，且原材料分布于世界各地。其二，当一个国家没有足够的某一特定商品来满足自身需求时，就需要有国际贸易。当一个国家的国内生产不足以满足其消费需求时就必须进口。其三，某国销售产品的成本较其他国家更低。最后，技术革新或产品的款式变化也会导致国际贸易的产生。

每个国家都需进口其自身不生产的货物和商品，并且得挣外汇来支付进口。于是该国通过出口其制成品和过剩原材料来挣取外汇。因此进口贸易和出口贸易是同一事物的两个方面，两者皆可对国内市场产生有利影响。进口商品给国产商品带来竞争；出口则给生产者提供更大的市场，从而有利于降低国内市场商品的价格。

但是,也有一些因素迫使各国政府对外贸加以限制。为了保护国内某一工业或者为了用有限的外汇来购买更急需的商品,政府可能对进口加以控制或征收关税。同样,为了保护国内某一正在发展的工业所需要的某一特定原材料,其出口也会受到限制。

Exercises

Part 1   Reading Comprehension

Directions:*Answer the following questions according to the text.*

1. In today's complex economic world, neither individuals nor nations are self-sufficient. Nations have utilized different economic resources; people have developed different skills.

2. First, no nation has all of the commodities that it need and raw materials are scattered around the world. Second, international trade occurs when a country does not have enough of a particular item to meet its needs. It often consumes more than it can produce internally and thus must import. Third, one nation can sell some items at a lower cost than other countries. Finally, international trade takes place because of innovation or style.

3. The import and export trades are two sides of the same coin, and both can have beneficial effects on the home market. Imports create competition for home-produced goods; exporting gives a manufacturer a larger market for his products, so helping to reduce the unit cost. In each case the effect is to keep prices in the home market down.

4. Imports may be controlled or subjected to a customs duty to protect a home industry, or because the available foreign exchange has to be channeled into buying more essential goods. And exports, too, may be restricted, to conserve a particular raw material required by a developing home industry.

Part 2   Words & Structure

Directions:*Choose the correct word form to fit into each sentence. Make proper changes where necessary.*

1. A. economic   B. economical   C. economy
2. A. source   B. resource   C. origin

3. A. competitive   B. competition   C. competing

4. A. effective   B. affects   C. effect

Part 3   Translation

1. Directions: *Translate the following passage into Chinese.*

　　一个具有宏伟发展计划的发展中国家,为有效地实行其发展计划,可能需要大量进口货物、技术、原材料和消费品及其他产品。由于进口依靠出口来融资,出口获得的外汇可用来进口急需的原材料、技术及设备,因此一个国家的进口能力显然取决于其出口业绩的好坏。

2. Directions: *Translate the following sentences into English.*

1) Neither you nor I am responsible for this.

2) To meet the increasing needs of people's life, we must vigorously expand social productive forces.

3) How much did you pay for the dictionary?

4) Imports and exports have both favorable and unfavorable effects on the home market.

5) Governments may sometimes place restrictions on imports of certain types of goods in order to protect some national industries.

Text B

参考译文

股　　票

　　股票的每一股代表着一家公司的一份股份。一家公司是由它的股票持有人(通常是成千上万的人和机构)所拥有,每一人或每一机构拥有公司的一小部分。

　　当你买进一家公司的股票时,你就成为公司的所有者或股东(亦称为持股人)。你随即拥有了公司所拥有的每一个建筑物,每一件办公家具和每一台机器的一部分,不论那一部分是如何之小。

　　作为持股人,当公司盈利时你也可能获利,你可依法拥有在重大决策上发言的权利,诸如是否追加发行股票,将公司出售给外部的买家,或变更董事会。按规定每一股拥有相同的表决权。因此,你拥有的股份越多,你的权力就越大。

　　股市是具有周期的。它在经历了一段上升期后会进行自我反转,反之亦然。上升期被看作是一个多头市场(牛市)——多头是指那些能使价格上涨的市场乐观主义者。空头市场(熊市)是一个下跌的市场,在这里悲观主义者正在把价格搞得越来越低。

　　关于这些称谓的出处存在着许多流行的看法,一个通常的说法是这些术语体现了动物的进攻方式——熊在进攻时会用掌向下煽,而牛则是将犄角向上方挑。这是一个有用的记忆方式,但并不是真正的出处。

　　术语"空头"源自于那些在尚未捉到熊之前即把熊皮事先卖出而闻名的熊皮商。逐渐地,术语"空头"即指那些同意卖出手中并不拥有的股票的投机商。如果他们认为价格将会下跌,这些空头则同意在一定的价位卖出股票,继而,他们会在较低的价位迅速买进股票,并按事先同意的较高价位将股票卖出。当然,空头们是在赌价位将会下跌。

　　因为牛熊相斗曾一度是一种流行的玩笑,多头便因而被用来表示空头的对立面。多头是指那些大量买入股票并希望价格上涨的人。

Exercises

Part 1　Reading Comprehension

Directions:*Answer the following questions according to the text.*

1. A share of stock represents ownership in a corporation.

2. A corporation is owned by its stockholders—often thousands of people and institutions—each owning a fraction of the corporation.

3. When you buy stock in a corporation you become a part-owner or stockholder (also known as shareholder). You immediately own a part, no matter how small, of every building, piece of office furniture, machinery—whatever that company owns.

4. As a shareholder, you stand to profit when the company profits. You are also legally entitled to a say in major policy decisions, such as whether to issue additional stock, sell the company to outside buyers, or change the board of directors. The rule is that each share has the same voting power, so the more share you own, the greater your power.

5. The term bear is derived from bear skin jobbers who had a reputation for selling bear skins before the bears were caught.

Part 2   Words & Structure

Directions: *Choose the correct word form to fit into each sentence. Make proper changes where necessary.*

1. A. former   B. precious   C. previous
2. A. reversed   B. inverted
3. A. ordinary   B. universal   C. common

Part 3   Translation

1. Directions: *Translate the following passage into Chinese.*

这些因素中有些是经济方面的；经济中的生产力水平、利息率和汇率。充裕的货币供应会刺激所有形式的投资；紧缩的货币供应者会使各类投资受到抑制。税率的变动也可以对股票购买方式产生影响。

2. Directions: *Translate the following sentences into English.*

1) His father owns some stock in that highway.

2) He has only done a fraction of his homework.

3) He is entitled to give a speech to those college students.

4) The stock price trends upward for periods of time, then reverse itself, and vice versa.

5) Many English words are derived from Latin.

Writing Practice

Directions: *You are asked to write in more than 120 words about the title of "The Changing of Chinese University Students' Spare Time".* The table below shows the average hours spent by Chinese university students in their spare time each day from 1999 to 2003 according to the statistics issued by Newspaper of China Youth. Describe and explain the information shown in the table in your own words. You should base your composition on the outline given below:

Average hours spending	1999	2000	2001	2002	2003
Part-time jobs	1	1	1.5	2	2
Internet-surfing	0.5	0.5	1	2	3
Clubs and society	2	1.5	1	0.5	0.5
Sports	2.5	3	2	1.5	0.5
Sleeping	8	8	7.5	6.5	6
Total spare time (hour)	14	14	13	12.5	12

Average hours spent by Chinese university students in their spare time each day

1. 上图所示为 1999 年至 2003 年中国大学生平均业余时间的安排情况,请描述其变化。

2. 请说明造成这些变化的原因(可以从大学生的学习,就业和经济压力以及因特网的广泛使用等方面加以说明)。

Sample

The Changing of Chinese University Students' Spare Time

The table shows the average number of hours Chinese college students spend on the five aspects, namely, part-time jobs, Internet surfing, clubs and societies, sports and sleeping in their free time between 1999 and 2003. It can be clearly seen that the total amount of spare time available decreased gradually and that the time they spent on their leisure activities and sleeping varied considerably in that span of time.

According to the figures, while, on average, the students could spend strikingly more time on Internet and slightly more on part-time jobs, they could only afford less time on the extracurricular activities such as clubs and societies and sports, which both dropped dramatically. And they sleep two hours less now than four or five years ago.

A number of factors could account for those changes. First the current college students are under much heavier pressure of study due to the ever-keener competition in the employment market. Next, there is growing number of positions and varieties of part-time jobs available for the students ranging from acting as tutors, interpreters to technicians. And finally, they tend to immerse themselves into Internet due to its prevalence in the recent years.

(196 words)

Further Practice

Part 1 Multiple Choice

Directions: *There are 10 incomplete sentences in this part. For each sentence there are four choices marked **A**, **B**, **C** and **D**. Choose the **ONE** that best completes the sentence.*

1~5 C A A B D   6~10 C B D B D

Part 2 Cloze

Directions: *Fill in the blanks with the proper words.*

(1) living   (2) for   (3) it   (4) of   (5) they

(6) The   (7) and   (8) is   (9) highly   (10) system

Part 3 Reading Comprehension

Directions: *Choose the best answer after reading the following passage.*

1~5 C C A C B

Unit 10 *Computer*

Key & Difficult Points：(重点、难点)

New Words

online, fantasy, bookworm, insulate, quantity, compute, operate, assistance, translate, dictate, relieve, routine, physical, figure, artificial, intelligence, unique, species, gift, develop, discovery, summary, reporter, ability, extraordinary

Phrases & Expressions

in a rush, pain in the neck, up to someone, take a look at, be connected with, nothing but, take over, a series of, relieve...of, put ideas together, look to, look at, be useful to, with the help of

Exercises

Listening Practice：Section A(Exercises 1,2)

Reading Practice：**Text A**　Part 2　Words & Structure (Exercises 1,2)

Part 3　Translation (Exercise 2)

Text B　Part 2　Words & Structure (Exercises 1,2)

Part 3　Translation (Exercise 2)

Writing Practice

Further Practice：Part 1　Multiple Choice

Part 2　Cloze

Listening Practice

Section A

Key to

Exercise 1

Directions: *Listen to the conversations and choose the best answer to complete each of the following statements.*

1~5 A D D C C

Tape-script

1. W: How do you usually come to work, Mr. Smith?
   M: Well, I usually drive.

2. M: What are you doing with that camera?
   W: Smile, I want a picture of you.

3. W: I need to catch the bus, and it leaves at 10:30.
   M: You'd better hurry. It's already 10:15.

4. M: How much are these shirts?
   W: They are on sale today, sir. Twenty -five dollars each, or two for forty dollars.

5. W: Where on earth are we?
   M: Judging by the traffic, I'd say we're near the heart of the city.

Exercise 2

Directions: *Listen to the dialogue and choose the best answer to each of the following questions.*

1~3 C B A

Tape-script

Dad: Do you remember our old computer?

Mom: How could I forget it? I don't ever want to see that old dinosaur again.

Dad: Oh, come on.

Mom: Really. It made me so frustrated.

Dad: Well, it's true that new computers are much, much better than the old ones. But still, it's hard for me to learn programs even on the new computers.

Mom: I know what you mean. You know, I've been thinking that maybe we should take an evening class. What do you think? We could get a babysitter.

Dad: That's great.

Section B

Key to

Exercise

Directions: *Complete the following dialogue according to what you hear.*

(1) surfing   (2) personally

(3) junk   (4) resist

(5) lure   (6) useful

(7) Google   (8) favorite

(9) prefer   (10) old-fashioned

Tape-script

Tom: Hey Max, what're you doing?

Max: I'm surfing the Net, of course. But it doesn't seem that easy to get what I want. There are always so many choices.

Tom: Yeah. I personally think that there's far too much junk on the Net.

Max: In my opinion, it doesn't really matter. But you need to learn to screen out the junk. Once you have used the Internet, you can't resist the lure of it.

Tom: Yeah, but to me, it's just a quick way of sending e-mail.

Max: You may try some search engines, and you will find that the Internet is very useful. Have you tried Google? It's my favorite.

Tom: Google? Well, to tell the truth, I haven't.

Max: It's a great search engine. It seems to be able to give me more of the right kind of information.

Tom: As far as I'm concerned, I still prefer the old-fashioned way—going to the library, you know, for books.

Oral Practice

参考译文

对话 1

情景

汤姆和简是朋友。最近简去了佛罗里达，走之前给汤姆发了电子邮件，但汤姆没有看到。这期间汤姆给简打过几次电话但没人接。一天，他们偶然相遇，汤姆问简是怎么回事。

汤姆：嗨，简。我们好久没见了。给你打过几次电话都没人接。

简： 你没收到我发的电子邮件吗？我和室友开车去佛罗里达旅游了，我们在那儿呆了两周。

汤姆：抱歉，马克斯一直占着电脑。

简： 噢，没关系，汤姆。他是不是一直在线聊天？

汤姆：是的。我都不敢相信他在那上面花了那么多时间。我觉得他是在虚幻的网络里浪费时间。

简： 嗯，至少他在和人们交流，在和其他地方的人交朋友。

汤姆：简，问题是我们在这个城市里可以接触到世界各地的人。

对话 2

情景

汤姆和杰克是朋友，他们在不同的公司工作。一天，汤姆在上班的路上看到了行色匆匆的杰克。

汤姆：我希望没有打扰你,你好像很忙?

杰克：如果不赶快去工作,会有麻烦的。我的工作很令我头痛。我总是有很多任务,而且老板的脾气很坏。

汤姆：你那么喜欢读书,怎么不回学校念书? 你可以学点新东西,再重新找份工作。

杰克：你认为我做什么好?

汤姆：看你自己吧。

杰克：计算机或许不错。

汤姆：好主意。计算机运用得很广泛。把它学好你就能找到一份好工作。

杰克：我会考虑的。哦,我得走了。以后再给你打电话。再见。

汤姆：再见。

Reading Practice

Text A

参考译文

计算机能思考吗?

首先让我们来看一下人脑。人脑包含着数十亿的神经细胞,由纤细的神经相互连接着。电脉冲沿着这些神经流过,很像电流通过绝缘的电线。神经在哪里相遇,哪里就会出现像电开关一样的小连接点。

计算机和人脑相似,它由很小的部件组成,这些部件像人脑的神经细胞一样工作。它们由电线连接。另外还有一些小开关能阻止电脉冲通过或让其通过。计算机像人脑,它也有一个存储器,能储存大量资料,例如可以把整个图书馆的资料储存在里面。

计算机还能做其他什么工作呢? 早期的计算机只能做加减乘除的运算。今天有些计算机仍然在做这样的工作。但现代计算机事实上能做的事还多得多。例如,它能操纵一个化工厂而不需要人辅助;能控制宇宙飞船飞往月球;它能阅读;还能以每分钟 2000 个词的速度把一种语言译成另一种语言,它甚至还能打出你口述的信件,并且用你所选择的任何语言打出。

任何一连串不断重复的活动几乎都可以由计算机来承担。计算机将逐步使人从一切单调无味的日常脑力或体力劳动中解放出来,使他有时间从事更高级的脑力劳动。

计算机能思考吗？回答是也能，也不能。这取决于什么叫思考。计算机能比任何人脑更好地处理数字。可是人脑可以做更多的工作，它可以用各种方法去整理思路，并提出以前没有人想到过的新的想法。具有数十亿的神经细胞的人脑仍然是一种比任何计算机都要卓越得多的结构。

Exercises

Part 1　Reading Comprehension

Directions：*Decide whether the following statements are true or false according to the text. Write "**T**" for True and "**F**" for False.*

1~5　T　F　F　T　T

Part 2　Words & Structure

1. Directions：*Match an expression in **Column B** which is similar in meaning to the **ONE** in **Column A**.*

1)~5)　e　h　b　a　d　　　　6)~10)　c　f　i　j　g

2. Directions：*Fill in each of the blanks with an appropriate word or phrase from the box. Change the form if necessary.*

1) A series of　　　　　　2) ideas

3) Take a look at　　　　　4) mental

5) Nothing but　　　　　　6) dull

7) leave　　　　　　　　　8) rate

9) wire　　　　　　　　　10) consists of

Part 3　Translation

1. Directions：*Translate the following sentences into Chinese.*

1) 计算机像人脑，它也有一个存储器，能储存大量资料。

2) 早期的计算机只能做加减乘除的运算。

3) 任何一连串不断重复的活动几乎都可以由计算机来承担。

4) 计算机将逐步使人从一切单调无味的日常脑力或体力劳动中解放出来，使他有时间从事更高级的脑力劳动。

5) 具有数十亿的神经细胞的人脑是一种比任何计算机都要卓越得多的结构。

2. Directions: *Translate the following sentences into English.*

1) The two towns are connected by a railway.

2) Your opinion is similar to mine.

3) I've warned you over and over again not to do that.

4) She came up with a new idea for increasing sales.

5) The general was relieved of his command.

Text B

参考译文

人与计算机：一种工作关系

机器能和人一样聪明吗？目前有很多关于人工智能机器以及它们与人类智力之间关系的讨论。

人类是一个独特的种类。他们有语言天赋并且能够相互交流思想、观念和情感。人对往事感兴趣并从中吸取经验。他们仔细研究当前的问题，然后决定怎么做。他们展望未来并制定下一步活动计划。他们发明工具和机器以辅助自己的劳动。

一些电脑学家正在研制一种据说可以像人一样思维的人工智能机器。据这些科学家说，这种电脑懂得书面语和口语以及相关的概念。它们能纠正自己所犯的错误，能用不止一种方法思考问题并选择一个最佳解决办法。它们还能利用信息计划未来，甚至能编程或教别的电脑成为它们的助手。

将来，对于从事不同职业的人来说，人工智能电脑将会非常有用。医生会利用它们来发现更多有关病人疾病的情况。地理学家可以借助电脑发现新的石油，其他矿物质，甚至化石。电脑可编程为新闻记者写摘要。律师还可以利用电脑这个助手来找到解决问题的更好方法。目前电脑每秒可以执行二亿四千万个指令，不久电脑每秒将可以执行十亿个指令。

人类能发明使生活更加便利的东西，人工智能电脑就是其中一例。这些机器可以做许多事情，而且做得比人类更好、更快。将来，电脑的工作方式将会更加不同凡响。但它们不会比为它们编程的人类更聪明。人类同电脑将会有一个良好的工作关系。

Exercises

Part 1　Reading Comprehension

Directions: *Choose the best answer according to the text.*

1~5　D　B　D　C　D

Part 2　Words & Structure

1. Directions: *Match an expression in **Column B** which is similar in meaning to the **ONE** in **Column A**.*

1)~5)　f　a　b　h　j　　　　6)~10)　e　d　g　c　i

2. Directions: *Fill in each of the blanks with an appropriate word or phrase from the box. Change the form if necessary.*

1) is interested in　　　　2) summary

3) found out　　　　　　4) at present

5) species　　　　　　　6) intelligent

7) as much as　　　　　8) look at

9) related to　　　　　　10) learn from

Part 3　Translation

1. Directions: *Translate the following paragraph into Chinese.*

　　人类是一个独特的种类。他们有语言天赋并且能够相互交流思想、观念和情感。人对往事感兴趣并从中吸取经验。他们仔细研究当前的问题,然后决定怎么做。他们展望未来并制定下一步活动计划。他们发明工具和机器以辅助自己的劳动。

2. Directions: *Translate the following sentences into English.*

1) Everything went according to plan.

2) With the help of his classmates he has made great progress.

3) This dictionary is very useful to English learning.

4) Who knows what will happen in the future?

5) There are two more students today than yesterday.

Writing Practice

Directions: *Write a composition on the topic : **"Will Computer Replace Us?"** You should write at least 120 words.*

Sample

Will Computer Replace Us?

As is the case we can see, the rapid development of computer technology is exerting profound impact on our life, almost in every aspect. They are so intelligent that they seem to be able to solve all problems; consequently, some say that it will sooner or later take the place of human beings.

As for me, I hold the view that computers are machines made by humans and they can only do as humans instruct them. For human, there is one thing that computers can never accomplish, that is, the former can make decision by their own while the latter can do nothing unless they are programmed. In spite of the remarkable skill of the computer, men can never become its slave.

In a word, computers will remain nothing but an extension of human brains, no matter how clever and sophisticated they will become.

(148 words)

Further Practice

Part 1　Multiple Choice

Directions: *There are 10 incomplete sentences in this part. For each sentence there are four choices marked **A**, **B**, **C** and **D**. Choose the **ONE** that best completes the sentence.*

1~5　A　C　B　C　D　　　　　6~10　B　B　A　D　D

Part 2　Cloze

Directions: *There are 10 blanks in the following passage. For each blank there* *are four choices marked* **A**, **B**, **C**, *and* **D**. *You should choose the* **ONE** *that best fits into the passage.*

1~5　D　A　A　D　B　　　　6~10　C　B　C　D　C

Part 3　Reading Comprehension

Directions: *Choose the best answer after reading the following passage.*

1~4　A　C　C　B

Public Practical English

（Book Two）

Unit 1 *Food & Party*

Key & Difficult Points:(重点、难点)

New Words

juice, cereal, bacon, brand, delicious, president, banquet, host, conversation, premier, immerse, trifle, inquire, course, establish, minor, detail, sausage, fry, crisp, passion, tray, supermarket, spread

Phrases & Expressions

enjoy oneself, How about..., show off, set an example, pay attention to, seize upon, let out, followed one's example, in company with, in most cases, in particular, specialize in, as 引导状语从句的用法, "no + -er + than ...", self-构成的合成词

Exercises

Listening Practice:Section A(Exercise)
Reading Practice: **Text A**   Part 2   Words & Structure (Exercise 1, 2)
                                 Part 3   Translation (Exercise 2)
                  Text B   Part 2   Words & Structure (Exercise 1)
                                 Part 3   Translation (Exercise 2)
Further Practice:Part 1   Multiple Choice

Listening Practice

Key to

Exercise

Directions: *In this section, you will hear 6 short conversations. At the end of each conversation, a question will be asked about what was said. Listen carefully and choose the best answer.*

1~6 C B B A A D

Tape-script

1. W: How is George doing at the moment?

   M: He's doing fine. He planned to change his job for a while but finally decided to keep the present one.

   Q: What can we learn about George in this conversation?

2. W: If I were you I'd live in the city instead of commuting to work by train.

   M: But the country is so beautiful in the spring and fall.

   Q: Where does the man prefer to live?

3. W: May I see the menu, please? I've been waiting an hour already.

   M: Here you are, Madam. I'll be back for your order in just a minute.

   Q: Where does this conversation take place?

4. M: Mrs. Hunter, you must take three pills every five hours without fail. And don't forget to finish the bottle.

   W: Don't worry, Doctor. I want to get well as quickly as I can.

   Q: What will the woman probably do?

5. M: Oh dear. I got home very late last night. I hope I didn't disturb you.

   W: No, I didn't hear a thing.

   Q: What can you conclude from this conversation?

6. W: Would you like to have dinner with me next Saturday?

   M: That's Saturday, July 2nd. Thank you very much, but I'm afraid I won't be able to. I'm going to the theater that evening.

Q: What is the man going to do next Saturday evening?

Section B

Key to

Exercise 1

Directions: *In this section, you will hear a passage. At the end of the passage, there are some questions. Listen carefully and choose the best answer.*

1~3 C D A

Tape-script

Directions: *In this section, you will hear a passage. At the end of the passage, there are some questions. Listen carefully and choose the best answer.*

A Chinese student went to study in England. His surname was Sun. it spelt S-U-N, just like the sun in the sky spelt S-U-N. England is a country with bad weather. The people there don't get much sunshine in the year.

When the Chinese student arrived at London Airport, a tall England policeman with a long face opened his passport to check the visa. The policeman was interested to find the Chinese name "Sun" in the passport. He thought it was pronounced just like the English word "Sun". So he said to the student, "I see your name is Sun. You are wanted here. "

The Chinese student was greatly surprised because if you are wanted by the police, you must have broken a law. So he asked the policeman: "Is there anything wrong with my passport or the visa? Do I have to go back?"

"Go back?" shouted the policeman. "Now that you're here, we'll never let you go away. "

The young man was very surprised. He thought he was going to be arrested. He was quite sure now that he had broken a law. He asked again: "What's happened? What have I done?"

It was only then that the policeman began to smile: "You don't know what you've done, Mr. Sun? You've brought sunshine to England. So we don't want you to go away. "

Questions:

1. What was the policeman interested in?
2. What do you think of that policeman?
3. What had the student thought at first?

Exercise 2

Directions: *In this section, you will hear a conversation. This conversation contains many of the most common verbs used in recipes or when talking about cooking food. Listen carefully and put the missing verbs in the blanks.*

(1) pool	(2) wash	(3) slice	(4) Rinse	(5) put
(6) Get	(7) pour	(8) Heat	(9) add	(10) Fry
(11) heat	(12) shake	(13) place	(14) Leave	(15) turn

Tape-script

Directions: *In this section, you will hear a conversation. This conversation contains many of the most common verbs used in recipes or when talking about cooking food. Listen carefully and put the missing verbs in the blanks.*

Speaker 1: Hi, Chris. I have some friends born England coming round for a meal this evening. I want to buy and make something Western for them.

Speaker 2: You say they're from England? Why don't you make steak and French Fries? That's popular in England.

Speaker 1: Ok, that sounds good. So, how do I make it?

Speaker 2: Easy. Go and buy some nice pieces of steak. You'll also need some garlic, salt and black pepper. Of course you'll also need some large potatoes. Oh, and you'll also need quite a lot of cooking oil.

Speaker 1: Ok, so once I have everything I need, what do I do?

Speaker 2: Well, the first thing to do is to peel and wash the potatoes. Then you slice the potatoes into long, quite thin strips. Rinse the pieces of potato again and then put them to one side.

Speaker 1: Ok, that's easy so far. What do I do next?

Speaker 2: Get a large handling pan and pour a little oil into it. Heat the oil in the pan and then add some garlic. Fry the garlic for a few minutes. While you are doing this，pour some oil into another pan and heat it. This oil needs to be very hot. Now，shake a little salt on both sides of the steaks and put them into the pan. Carefully place the pieces of potato into the hot oil. Leave the potato to cook for about ten minutes or so.

Speaker 1：Easy. What about the steaks? What do I do with them while the French Fries are cooking?

Speaker 2：Nothing much. When they have been cooking for a minute or so，turn them all over. Remember，you can ask your guests how they like their steaks cooked. Some people like them to be cooked longer than others.

Speaker 1：Well，that sounds really easy! What do you think I should serve this with?

Speaker 2：You could steam or boil some vegetables，but I think a salad is probably the easiest to prepare.

Oral Practice

参考译文

对话 1

情景

　　贝克先生和他的女朋友去一家餐馆吃饭。一个侍者走过来热情地为他们服务。

侍者：您要点什么，先生？

贝克：今天你们这儿有什么？

侍者：有果汁、酒、蛋糕、点心和各种东西。

贝克：我想为我朋友要一杯番茄汁。

侍者：要些谷类食品吗，先生？

贝克：是的，要一盘小麦片。

侍者：还要蛋类食品吗？

贝克：是的，要熏猪肉和鸡蛋配着奶油的土司面包。我想要我的熏猪肉做得脆点。

侍者：鸡蛋要做成什么样的？

贝克：油煎的。

侍者：还要别的吗，先生？

贝克：不要，够了。谢谢。

对话 2

情景

今天是劳动节，托马斯请他的中国朋友李先生与他的家人一块吃饭。下面是他们的谈话：

托马斯：李先生请进。见到你很高兴。

李先生：抱歉我来晚了。

托马斯：哦，没关系。你能来我们很高兴。晚餐已准备好。请到餐桌就座吧。

李先生：非常感谢。

托马斯：这是我的妻子的拿手菜。

李先生：很好吃。

托马斯：让我们尝尝中国茅台酒吧。它非常出名。

李先生：是的。谢谢你。但是我不能再喝了。

托马斯：来些苹果馅饼怎么样？

李先生：好，只一块。

托马斯：你觉得怎么样？

李先生：它非同寻常，但说实话，我几乎饱了。哦，恐怕我该走了。谢谢你让我度过了一个美好的夜晚。

托马斯：不客气。非常感谢你的到来。我正在为你沏咖啡。

李先生：哦，不。我真地喝不下了。确实非常感谢。我今晚真得很快乐。我非常高兴你邀请我来。

托马斯：不用谢。好，那么我不再留你了。再见。

李先生：再次感谢。再见。

Reading Practice

Text A

参考译文

总统和筷子

克林顿也学习使用筷子，以便在北京的国宴上表演一番。

自尼克松 1972 年首次访华以来，每一位美国总统都访问过中国。学习使用筷子是重要一课，这不仅是饮食文化的一部分，也是政治艺术，是表现自己能力并博取主人欢心的"小动作"。

要重视筷子艺术，尼克松为美国总统做了个榜样，那也是他访问时在国宴上的话题。它和尼克松喝茅台酒的镜头一样，都是通过电视向全球播送的。从此美国总统访华，都力求表现使用筷子的技巧。

在 1972 年的宴会上，周恩来总理注意到尼克松总统使用筷子的手法，于是称赞他和夫人使用筷子技巧一流。尼克松夫人立即津津乐道，当场"泄密"，她说，为了来中国，他们在白宫一直学习使用筷子。原来，尼克松夫妇早在访华前半年，进餐时已不用刀叉，改用筷子。

对尼克松夫妇而言，他们使用筷子的技巧被主人称赞，是最开心的一件事。政治家融入到访国家的文化而受赞赏，是最成功和最有面子的事情。

别看使用筷子这雕虫小技，西方人想要不出错，需要苦练多时。尼克松总统对此事一丝不苟。他曾向巴基斯坦总统打听，北京国宴用哪一类筷子，通常有多少道菜等，然后他用类似的筷子认真练习和彩排。

尼克松首次访华，双方未建交，不是正式国事访问。尽管如此，他即使对小节也不马虎。以后美国总统访问中国，模仿他的做法，特别是细节上的安排。

Exercises

Part 1   Reading Comprehension

Directions: *Choose the best answer according to the text.*
1)～5) D C A D B

2. Directions: *Answer the following questions according to the text.*

1) Mrs. Nixon immediately seized up on the topic with great relish and even let out the "secret".

2) Before they visited China, they had been practicing using chopsticks in the White House.

3) President Nixon had taken the matter very seriously.

4) Nixon practiced with similar chopsticks and held dress rehearsals.

Part 2   Words & Structure

1. Directions: *Match an expression in Column B, which is similar in meaning to the one in Column A.*

1)~5) e h j c b   6)~10) i a g f d

2. Directions: *Fill in each of the blanks with an appropriate word or phrase from the box. Change the form if necessary.*

1) detail

2) praised

3) appears

4) showing off

5) cultures

Part 3   Translation

1. Directions: *Translate the following passage into Chinese.*

　　自从 1972 年以后，使用筷子是美国人访问中国之前都要学习一门重要技术。他们认为使用筷子不仅是中国文化的一部分，而且也是一种政治艺术。通过在该国展示使用筷子的"小计"，他们能赢得主人的快乐并有助于改善两个国家之间的关系。那就是他们为什么要对看上去较小的细节，像这种吃饭的方法给予特别的注意。

2. Directions: *Translate the following sentences into English.*

1) When you read, please pay attention to your pronunciation.

2) We should give children more praise and less criticism.

3) He'd like to show off his old achievements on the banquets.

4) It is not easy to master a foreign language.

5) The moment/ As soon as the thief put his hand in a passenger's pocket, he

was seized upon by the police.

Text B

美国食品

汉堡包和热狗应该是最为熟知的美国食品了。热狗,一种把香肠夹在面包中的食物,在小吃店或街边的热狗摊上随处可见。从旧金山到纽约,中小饭店,汉堡包都会和牛排、炸鸡以及海鲜一起出现在菜单上。通常,当然都会物有所值。在美国食物里还会提供些点心,比如,苹果派、起司蛋糕、巧克力蛋糕、冰淇淋及圣代冰淇淋。世界上,没有比美国冰淇淋更好吃的了。

美国人追求速度的激情也在影响着它的食品业。许多饭店,尤其是像麦当劳之类的大型专业快餐连锁店,柜台上提供立等可取的食物。在美国还有一些"免下车"快餐店,人们不下车就可以买饭。有的人喜欢在餐桌上吃饭,他们一般也使用纸杯和塑料容器,刀、叉、和勺子也是塑料的。吃完之后,他们只需把托盘上的东西倒进垃圾桶即可。

在大大小小的多数城市,你都可以找到墨西哥或者意大利食品。即使是小城的咖啡店也提供一些简单的食品以及各种饮料,当然也包括新鲜、极致的咖啡。你可在吧台上享用,也可以在桌旁细斟。

大多数美国家庭都为自己的厨艺而骄傲,他们大都有大容量冰箱,可以把从超级市场或农园弄来的食物储藏起来。超级市场是大型自助式的店铺,里面有各种新鲜、罐装或冷冻的食品。所以,像快食店一样,比一般市场要方便便宜。超级市场出现在美国的 19 世纪 30 年代,现在它已经进入世界大部分地区。

Exercises

Part 1   Reading Comprehension

1. Directions:*Choose the best answer according to the text.*
1)~5) A A D A A

2. Directions:*Answer the following questions according to the text.*
1) We can buy hot dogs in snack bars and from hot dog stands on street corners.

2) American ice cream.

3) No，they throw everything except the tray into a trash can.

4) Supermarkets are large self-service stores selling every kind of food — fresh，canned or frozen. So like the fast-food restaurants，their produce is less expensive and easier to market.

5) Open.

Part 2 Words & Structure

1. Directions：*Match an expression in* **Column B** *which is similar in meaning to the one in* **Column A**.

1)～5) d g j c h   6)～10) i a e f b

2. Directions：*Choose the correct meaning for the italicized words*.

1～5 A B A B B

Part 3 Translation

1. Directions：*Translate the following passage into Chinese*.

你喜欢美国食物吗？

（琳达和刘玲在美国是同班同学，现在他们正谈论食物。）

琳达：告诉我，玲，你喜欢美国食物？

刘玲：哦，不。我真正喜欢的是我母亲的烹饪。我很想吃母亲做的饭菜！

琳达：最近你的体重一定减了。

刘玲：没有，我体重在增加！我想是我吃了许多垃圾食品的问题。

琳达：你的意思是巧克力，炸薯条，马铃薯片……这样的食品吗？

刘玲：是的，类似这些。而且美国人早餐吃甜食！并放许多糖！

琳达：是的。专家说那非常不健康。

刘玲：我过去在家几乎从不吃这些东西。我们国家有真正好吃的食品。

琳达：在美国，有各种餐馆，像中国餐馆，墨西哥餐馆，意大利餐馆……你可进行尝试。

刘玲：但我没有充足的时间。我总是很忙。通常在学校自助餐厅吃。

2. Directions：*Translate the following sentences into English*.

1) I give you my word of honor that I did not take the money.

2) He accepted her apology very graciously.

3) They still have a comfortable lead over their matches.

4) She looks much prettier with long hair than with short hair.

5) We have made informal approaches to the committee.

Writing Practice

Directions: *For this part you are asked to write a composition. The title of your composition is " **Fast Food in China** ". Your composition may include the following main ideas given in Chinese.*

Sample

Fast Food in China

Nowadays, there are two kinds of fast food in China: Chinese-style fast food and western-style fast food. They both have their advantage and disadvantages.

Western fast food industry has a longer history and more advanced management than its Chinese counterpart. Ever since they entered the Chinese market, the manufacturers have been successfully adjusting their products to the taste of the Chinese people, which are now popular with the children and the young.

Chinese fast food, however, suits the Chinese taste better and finds general support from all ages. Successful examples are Yong He Bean Mild and Grandma's Boiled Dumplings. Unfortunately, some Chinese fast food restaurant are ill managed, the tables and chairs being greasy and dirty, flies humming around, and the waiters looking indifferent and impatient, which drives away quite a lot of customers.

As a Chinese, I take pride in our age-old colorful food culture. I hope our fast food industry will absorb the advanced experience of western countries, and get the upper hand in the fierce competition.

(169 words)

Further Practice

Part 1 Multiple Choice

Directions: *There are 10 incomplete sentences in this part. For each sentence there are four choices marked **A**, **B**, **C** and **D**. Choose the **ONE** that best completes the sentence.*

1~5 A D B A A 6~10 A A D B C

Part 2 Cloze

Directions: *There are 10 blanks in the following passage. For each blank there are four choices marked **A**, **B**, **C** and **D**. Choose the **ONE** that best fits into the passage.*

1~5 B A C C D 6~10 C B A D B

Part 3 Reading Comprehension

Directions: *Choose the best answer after reading the following passage.*

1~3 C B A

Unit 2   *Choices*

Key & Difficult Points：(重点、难点)

New Words

admire，civilization，system，press，own，chief，enormous，self-confidence，assignment，recall，evaluate，tough，honest，fulfil，profession，ambition，talent，devote，achieve，identify，destroy，inspire，coach，explanation，punishment，goal，drawback，rainbow

Phrases & Expressions

show sb. around，as far as ... be concerned，make progress，catch up with，make an effort，cut off，turn in，have no idea of，dream of，start off，pay off，devote ... to，concentrate on，back up，give up，合成形容词，used to (do)表示过去常常的用法，表示将来情况的常用形式，co-作前缀常表示的意义，虚拟条件 if 省略从句倒装的情况，现在分词作状语的用法。

Exercises

Listening Practice：Section A(Exercise 1)
Section B(Exercise)
Reading Practice：**Text A**   Part 2   Words & Structure (Exercise 1, 2)
                      Part 3   Translation (Exercise 2)
           Text B   Part 2   Words & Structure (Exercise 2)
                      Part 3   Translation (Exercise 2)
Further Practice：Part 1   Multiple Choice
                Part 2   Cloze
                Part 3   Reading Comprehension

Listening Practice

Section A

Key to

Exercise 1

Directions: *Listen to a story and complete the summary below with the information you hear. Then write one word in each blank.*

(1) rich   (2) stone   (3) find   (4) effort   (5) passed

(6) on   (7) same   (8) about   (9) trouble   (10) pushed

(11) pulled   (12) move   (13) bag   (14) money   (15) removes

Exercise 2

Directions: *Listen to the story again and answer the following questions by filling in the missing words.*

1. What did the farmer think about the person who put the stone in the center of the road?

   He thought the person was <u>foolish</u>.

2. How would you describe the young man who removed the stone?

   He was <u>kind-hearted</u> and <u>hardworking</u>.

3. What did the young man worry about when he saw the stone?

   He was worried that other people would stumble on the stone and <u>hurt</u> <u>themselves</u>.

4. Where were the bag and the message?

   They were <u>under the stone</u>.

5. Who do you think put the money and the message there?

   <u>The rich man</u>.

Tape-script

Many years ago, there lived a rich man who wished to do something for the people of his village. First, however, he wanted to find out whether they deserved his help.

In the center of the main road into the village he placed a very large stone.

126

Then he hid nearby and waited to see what would happen. Soon an old farmer passed with his cow.

"What fool put this big stone right in the center of the road?" said the farmer, but he made no effort to remove the stone. Instead, with some difficulty he passed around the stone and continued on his way. Another man came along, and the same thing happened; then another came, and another, etc. All of them complained about the stone in the center of the road, but not one of them took the time and troubles to remove it.

Then came a young man, who was kind-hearted and hardworking. He saw the stone and said to himself, "It will be dark soon. Strangers or neighbors will come along in the dark, stumble on the stone, and perhaps hurt themselves."

The young man then began to remove the stone. He had to push and pull with all his strength to move it to one side. But imagine his surprise when under the stone, he found a bag full of money and this message: "This money is for the thoughtful person who removes this stone from the road. That person deserves help."

Section B

Key to

Exercise

Directions: *Listen to a story twice and complete each sentence with the best choice.*
1~5 A A B C B

Tape-script

One day a rich woman lost her handbag. There was a lot of money in it. So she made a promise: "If anybody finds my handbag and returns it to me, I'll give half the money to him."

A poor farmer found the handbag at a street corner. He sent it back to the loser. But the rich woman changed her mind.

"There was still an expensive watch in my handbag," said the loser, "I won't give half the money in my handbag to you until you return it to me."

"I've never seen an expensive watch in the handbag," said the farmer.

They began to quarrel. The rich woman wouldn't do what she had promised. The farmer became angry and took her to a judge.

After the judge heard what had happened to them, he said to the woman, "I'm sure that you have lost a handbag, and that there was an expensive watch in it. But there is only a lot of money in this handbag. I don't think it's yours. Wait for some time. Maybe somebody will return your handbag to you." Then the judge turned to the farmer and said, "Take the handbag home. If the loser doesn't go to get it back in three days, it will be yours."

Oral Practice

参考译文

对话1

情景

史密斯先生是一个外国投资商,他正在中国进行实地考察。接待员杨林在带他参观之后,问他对该城市的印象。

杨　林：史密斯先生,你对我们城市的印象怎样?

史密斯：非常好。它现代化、美丽而干净。这里的人们非常热情。我真的羡慕你们悠久的历史和古老的文明。

杨　林：每个国家、每个民族都有它自己丰富的历史遗产。

史密斯：那是真实的,但中国的文明是世界最古老的文明之一。

杨　林：就通讯系统来说,我们仍然相当落后。我们必须学习你们国家先进的技术。

史密斯：在这一领域你们已经取得了快速的进步。

杨　林：但是要赶上世界上最先进的国家,我们需要更大的努力。

对话2

情景

波比的车在路上突然坏了,因此,他走进哈林的修车厂寻求帮助。

波:我的车烧坏了。嗨!(没人答应,波比按喇叭)嗨! 喂! 喂!(波比关掉了修车厂的音乐)

达:谁关了我的音乐? 你关了我的音乐。

波:你是哈林吗?

达:不,我是达瑞尔。

波:这地方是你的吗?

达:是的。

波:可是为什么却叫"哈林汽修"呢?

达:因为哈林以前是老板。

波:你能看看我的车吗? 我想应该是水箱管破了。

达:是你的水箱管。它是爆了。

波:这我知道。我刚刚告诉你的。

达:我说,老板,既然你知道得这么多,为什么不自个儿修呢?

波:要是我自己能修,你认为我会站在这儿和你费口舌吗? 你是修呢,还是我另请高明?

达:另请高明? 伙计,离这儿最近的汽修站得走 50 英里。那是市中心的老汽修厂……可三年前关了门,就这情况。

波:好了,我被困在这儿了。你满意了吧? 你究竟能修还是不能修?

达:好的,我能修。

波:好极了。好极了。

Reading Practice

Text A

参考译文

四字改变人生

鲍勃·格林

　　某些瞬间的东西,有时却常常令人久久不能忘怀。同样,有些话虽然对说的人来讲算不了什么,(但对听的人来讲)却具有深远的影响。

　　最近我从一个叫马尔科姆·达尔克夫的人那儿听说了一件事。达尔克夫今年

48 岁,他当职业作家已有 24 个年头了。下面就是达尔克夫告诉我的。

达尔克夫在伊利诺伊州的罗克艾兰上中学的时候非常胆怯害羞。他没有什么朋友,缺乏自信。1965 年 10 月的一天,英语老师鲁思·布劳克给班上布置了一项作业,当时同学们一直在看《杀死一只知更鸟》。现在要他们续写一章,作为该书的结尾。

达尔克夫完成了作业并交了上去。如今,达尔克夫已想不起自己当时写的具体内容了,也想不起当时布劳克老师给了自己多少分。但他却清楚地记得布劳克老师在他作业上批的四个字——"写得很好"。这四个他永远都不会忘记的字。

四个字。寥寥四个字却改变了达尔克夫的生活道路。

"在此之前我一直不了解自己,也不知道自己将来要干什么。"达尔克夫说。"看了布劳克老师的批语,我回家之后就写了一篇短篇小说。我以前做梦都想写小说,可一直不知道自己能不能写好。"

从那时起到学年结束,达尔克夫写了很多短篇小说,拿到学校给布劳克老师看。布劳克老师对达尔克夫加以鼓励赞扬,但又实事求是,严格要求。达尔克夫说:"布劳克老师的做法我真求之不得。"

(后来)达尔克夫被指定为校报的副编辑。达尔克夫的信心与日俱增,视野也开阔了,开始踏上通向成功和幸福的人生道路。达尔克夫坚信,如果没有布劳克老师在他作业上批下的这四个字,一切都会大为不同。

"写得很好!"

这寥寥四个字,却能改变一切。

Exercises

Part 1　Reading Comprehension

1. Directions: *Decide whether the following statements are true or false according to the text. Put "T" for True and "F" for False.*

1)~5)　T　F　T　T　F

2. Directions: *Answer the following questions according to the text.*

1) The four words "This is good writing."

2) Dalkoff can't remember the grade.

3) He wrote a short story when he was back home, something he had always dreamed of writing but never believed he could do.

4) Dalkoff is convinced that none of this would have happened had that woman

not written those four words in the margin of his paper.

5）Open.

Part 2 Words & Structure

1. Directions：*Match an expression in* **Column B** *which is similar in meaning to the one in* **Column A**.

1）～5） j i g h f   6）～7） e a c b d

2. Directions：*Choose the* **ONE** *that best completes the sentence according to the text.*

1）～5） A A C D D   6）～10） B B A B C

Part 3 Translation

1. Directions：*Translate the following passage into Chinese.*

机　　会

　　一些人认为机会是他们生活中最重要的部分,是通往成功之路。因此当他们看见朋友成功时,会抱怨他们没有足够的好运气获得这个机会。但是另一些人认为机会纯粹是运气,只要他们努力工作,具有知识和技能,到处都会有机会在等待他们。

　　虽然人们对待机会的态度不同,但是机会的确是重要的,并且没有人能忽视。它能使一个人成功。我们应该抓住一切有价值的机会,并充分利用它,否则除了悔恨和失望,就没有什么东西留下来陪伴我们。

　　但是我认为并不是机会本身决定一个人的成功或者失败。我想,机会对每个人都是公正的。为了抓住机会,我们需要知识、技能和经验。总之,机会是重要的但不是决定性的。

2. Directions：*Translate the following sentences into English.*

1）I can recall your saying that you were going to be a lawyer.

2）I believe that you will understand it in the future.

3）If you make a promise you should fulfill it.

4）John's success encouraged him to continue.

5）The students were busy writing notes in the margin of the book.

6）We were so moved that we couldn't help crying.

Text B

参考译文

刻苦努力：通往成功之路

约翰·E·安德森

什么让像康德利扎·赖斯这样的人登上事业的顶峰？是刻苦努力、严于律己和积极思考。

进取心和动力在任何领域都很重要。但是，与一些运动员、企业家、艺术家和年轻人广泛接触后，我了解到，任何一个领域里，能攀登上事业高峰的人未必都是天赋过人的人，而是努力，且加倍努力的人。

当然，要使刻苦努力真正得到回报，你必须提高工作效率。方法如下：

追逐梦想。你得有努力的方向。尽早地树立目标，接着全力以赴去实现。

合理安排时间。艰难的工作不是随意应付就可以的。要做出成效，就必须持之以恒、不折不扣、并有回报。

一步一个脚印。我与运动员和企业家们谈论过"百分之一法"。不要想一步登天，每一个阶段能比上一个阶段有百分之一的进步就行。

正确对待自己的弱点。将注意力集中到需要改善的方面，不要重复做那些已经做得得心应手的事情。

勤于回顾。不管是经营还是学习，你在每天晚上，甚至一节课结束，或者练习结束之后，都要去回顾一下，问自己我有什么收获？哪些方面还要继续努力？应该为明天做些什么准备？

犒劳自己。不管工作忙到什么程度，只要取得一点成绩，就犒劳犒劳自己。如果你完成了当天规定的工作，那么你就去看场电影。这么一个奖励会激励你更加努力地工作。

组织一个拉拉队。不管目标有多重要，独自一人干总是很苦的。你得有人助威，有人喝彩叫"好"。

英国小说家约瑟夫·康拉德说过："工作就是给自己提供发现自我的机会。"如果把干活看成是惩罚。你就永远不会达到目的。刻苦努力的过程确实充满了困难，充满了挫折，充满了痛苦，甚至有的时候你会想索性不干了。但是，每一次挫折都会给你带来新的收获。

刻苦努力是通往美好的必由之路。

Exercises

Part 1   Reading Comprehension

1. Directions： *Decide whether the following statements are true or false according to the text. Put "**T**" for True and "**F**" for False.*

1)～5)   F   F   T   T   T

2. Directions： *Answer the following questions according to the text.*

1) They are hard work，lots of discipline and positive thinking.

2) What have I accomplished? What needs more work? What should I prepare for tomorrow?

3) Open.

Part 2   Words & Structure

1. Directions： *Match an expression in **Column B** which is similar in meaning to the one in **Column A**.*

1)～5)   e   a   i   g   h   6)～10)   c   f   d   j   b

2. Directions： *Fill in each of the blanks with an appropriate word or phrase from the box. Change the form if necessary.*

1) regular   2) drive   3) the heights   4) set   5) direction

6) It was found 7) single   8) support   9) put in   10) drawback

Part 3   Translation

1. Directions： *Translate the following sentences into Chinese.*

1) 但是，与一些运动员、企业家、艺术家和年轻人广泛接触后，我了解到，任何一个领领域里，能攀登上事业高峰的人未必都是天赋过人的人，而是努力，且加倍努力的人。

2) 不要想一步登天，每一个阶段能比上一个阶段有百分之一的进步就行。

3) 不管是经营还是学习，你在每天晚上，甚至一节课结束，或者练习结束之后，都要去回顾一下，问自己我有什么收获？哪些方面还要继续努力？应该为明天做些什么准备？

4) 有的时候你会想索性不干了。但是，每一次挫折都会给你带来新的收获。

5）刻苦努力是通往美好的必由之路。

2. Directions：*Translate the following sentences into English*.

1）He has a wife and 3 children to support.

2）Nothing would stop me from achieving my ambition.

3）We prepared ourselves for the worst.

4）A big fire destroyed the forest

5）Children at the age of 6 can attend school.

Writing Practice

Directions：*Write a composition on the topic*：**"Silence Is Not Always Gold"**. *You should write at least 120 words according to the suggestions given below in Chinese*.

Sample

Silence Is Not Always Gold

"Silence is gold" is a popular saying in which many people hold belief. To these people speaking too much is not a good merit. However, if you always keep silent, you will probably miss many golden opportunities instead of obtaining the gold of silence.

Last week I read an article written by an office lady. The company where she worked scheduled a discussion concerning all important project. Every employee in company was asked to voice his or her opinion. Everyone except her was enthusiastic and eagerly contributed to the discussion. But when it came to her turn, she hesitated, fearful that her opinion would not be taken seriously. She chose to remain silent. Much to her surprise, her silence at the discussion was interpreted as a sign of incompetence. In the end, she lost her job.

(136 words)

Further Practice

Part 1　Multiple Choice

Directions: *There are 10 incomplete sentences in this part. For each sentence there are four choices marked* **A** , **B** , **C** *and* **D** . *Choose the* **ONE** *that best completes the sentence.*

1~5　A　C　C　A　A　　　　6~10　A　A　A　D　D

Part 2　Cloze

Directions: *There are 10 blanks in the following passage. For each blank there are four choices marked* **A** , **B** , **C** *and* **D** . *Choose the* **ONE** *that best fits into the passage.*

　1~5　A　C　D　C　D　　　　6~10　B　A　C　C　D
11~15　B　D　A　B　B　　　　16~20　C　A　C　D　A

Part 3　Reading Comprehension

Directions: *Choose the best answer after reading the following passage.*
1~5　B　A　B　C　D

Unit 3   *Love*

Key & Difficult Points: (重点、难点)

New Words

exaggerate，wonder，resolve，fashion，magic，grab，confused，insight，upset，tear，lay，worship，pure，possession，hug，hunt，obey，tumble，impel，flit，throb，lest，mourn

Phrases & Expressions

look like，call up，reach out，long for，tear at，instead of，at present，fall under one's eye，no more，bind with，pass by，as if 引导条件从句的用法，too … to do 的用法

Exercises

Listening Practice：Section A(Exercise 1,2)
Reading Practice：**Text A**　Part 2　Words &. Structure (Exercise 1, 2)
　　　　　　　　　　　　Part 3　Translation (Exercise 1,2)
　　　　　　　　　　Text B　Part 2　Words &. Structure (Exercise 1,2)
　　　　　　　　　　　　Part 3　Translation (Exercise 1)
Further Practice：Part 1　Multiple Choice
　　　　　　　　　Part 2　Cloze

Listening Practice

Key to

Exercise 1

Directions: *In this part, you will hear a dialogue between Jane and Sally about the kind of person they would choose as husband. Listen carefully and put a tick (√) beside the good qualities mentioned in the dialogue for an ideal husband.*

(√) A. hard-working   (√) F. good-tempered

(   ) B. respectable   (√) G. intelligent

(√) C. reliable   (   ) H. handsome

(   ) D. generous   (   ) I. health y

(√) E. humorous   (   ) J. considerate

Exercise 2

Directions: *Listen to the dialogue again and complete the following sentences.*

1. Sally would take into consideration his <u>personality</u> and <u>background</u> while choosing a husband.
2. Sally has a <u>terrible</u> temper herself.
3. According to Sally, a marriage can't work if both people are the <u>same</u>.
4. People who've been brought up in <u>different</u> environments think differently.
5. To Sally, it matters the least whether he has good <u>looks</u>.

Tape-script

What Kind of Man Would You Like to Marry?

Jane: What kind of man would you like to marry, Sally?

Sally: I suppose I'd have to take two things into consideration: his personality and his background.

Jane: What would you look for?

Sally: Well, he'd have to be intelligent — I can't stand stupid people. He'd have to be hardworking, reliable, and down to earth. I couldn't get along with someone who wasn't practical.

Jane: I like a man with a good sense of humor.

Sally: Oh, I do, too. He'd have to be good-natured. I have a terrible temper myself, and I don't think a marriage can work if both people are the same.

Jane: What did you mean when you said that background was important?

Sally: As far as I'm concerned, people who've been brought up in different environments think differently. They usually just can't understand each other well enough to get married.

Jane: Do you think that good looks are important?

Sally: In my opinion, that matters the least, though of course I couldn't marry an ugly man.

Section B

Key to

Exercise

Directions: *In this section, you will hear a passage. Listen carefully and fill in the blanks with the exact words you have just heard.*

(1) events
(2) happen
(3) marked
(4) main
(5) choice
(6) affected
(7) differs
(8) celebrated
(9) The proud parents receive congratulations and parents on behalf of the new-born.
(10) The young couple go through a special wedding ceremony and receive presents to help them set up their home.

Tape-script

Birth, marriage and death: these are the greatest events in a human's life.

Many things, good or bad, can happen to us in our lives. Yet there are three days which are usually marked by some special ceremony: the day we are born, the day we get married and the day we die. These are the three main things in life. We only have a choice in the second of these: we can choose choice or not to marry. But we have no choice in birth and death. All human beings are affected by these three things. The only thing that differs in each society is the way in which these are celebrated. Yet all societies share common characteristics. Birth is a time of joy. The proud parents receive congratulations and parents on behalf of the new-born. Marriage is also a time of joy. The young couple go through a special wedding ceremony and receive presents to help them set up their home. Death is a time of sorrow and is marked by a special ceremony and mourning. The dates of all three events are usually remembered.

Oral Practice

参考译文

对话 1

> **情景**
> 艾略特与爱莉森在一起工作四年了,艾略特总是偷偷地注意爱莉森。现在他觉得已经爱上了爱莉森。所以,他尝试与爱莉森接触并示爱意。

艾:爱莉森,你好。

爱:你好。呃,呃……

艾:我叫艾略特·里查兹。我们见过几次。

爱:是的,我想起来了。嗨,你好吗?

艾:我好极了。我是在夸张。我……我还行。呃,你看,我们在这儿一起工作有四年了。我总是注意到你,而且认为你像是一个很有趣的人。

爱:我可不知道我怎么有趣。

艾:呃,事实上,我不了解你,你也不了解我。所以我在想,我们是否能相互认识一下,也许我们有可能碰巧谈得来。所以我在想,我们是否找个时间喝杯咖啡,或者……

爱:谢谢你的好意。呃,可我在与别人约会。

艾:呃,当然了,你这样的姑娘不乏人爱。你……他真是个幸运儿。呃,听着,如果你和他谈不来的话,那么……

爱:谢谢你的厚爱。好吧。

艾:不用谢,我应该谢谢你。再见。

爱:好的,保重。再见。

对话 2

情景

杰瑞深爱艾丽丝,因此,他努力向艾丽丝表达他的感情,并向她求爱。

杰:我不知该说什么。我爱你。

艾:什么?

杰:我…… 我……,就好像决心要以某种传统的方式,每天给你打 1000 个电话,问你是否愿意嫁给我。你做的每件事都充满魔力。

艾:这些话都是歌里的,杰瑞。

杰:是的,我知道,我知道。你看,我很紧张。我只是随意抓住想到的第一句话——我知道这些话是歌里的,但我也了解自己的感受……

艾:杰瑞,我想你是有些糊涂了。今天是漫长的一天,而……

杰:我没有糊涂。我没有。你想知道……墙上的那幅画,那可能是……

艾:我,我想我们不该谈这些。

杰:不,我们应该谈。那是哲罗尼摩。是爱。爱情赋予你洞察力。爱情让你看到平常看不到的……我只知道第一次看到你我就爱上了你。

艾:杰瑞,不。不是的。你不爱我。

杰:我肯定我爱你。

艾:不。

杰:我真的不爱你吗?

艾:是的。

杰:我原以为……我还以为,你知道……我只是觉得也许……我原以为……(转身跑走)

艾:杰瑞。杰瑞。

Reading Practice

Text A

参考译文

麦琪的礼物

欧·亨利

"你把头发剪了?"吉姆问道,语调那么缓慢,仿佛是他经过最艰苦的思索之后尚未把显而易见的事实弄明白似的。

"我将它剪掉卖了,"黛拉说,"已经卖了,我告诉你——卖了,再也没了。今晚是圣诞夜,吉姆别生气(对我好些),因为这都是为了你。"

吉姆好像忽然从昏睡状态中清醒过来。他从大衣口袋拿出一个包裹扔在桌上。

"黛拉,别误会,"他说,"剪掉头发决不会使我就不那么喜欢我亲爱的妻子了。但是如果你打开那个包裹,你就会明白我为什么起初那么难过。

白皙而灵巧的手指撕扯着绳子打开包装纸。啊!此时,她发出一声狂喜的尖叫。很快又簌簌地落起泪来。

因为摆在眼前的是一套梳子——是好几个月来黛拉所羡慕的,摆在一个商店的橱窗里的那套梳子。多么漂亮的梳子,纯玳瑁做的,边上镶着珠宝——颜色恰好配她那秀发。她知道它们是非常昂贵的,对那套梳子她虽然心向神往,但是丝毫没有想过会得到它。而现在它们是她的了,头发却已经卖掉,梳子还有什么用呢。

可是她把它们紧紧地抱在胸前,最后她抬起泪汪汪的眼睛,含笑说道:"我的头发长得很快,吉姆!"

此刻,黛拉记起了别的东西大声叫道:"哦,哦!"

吉姆尚未看到他的美丽礼物呢。她热切地将礼物托在自己的手上递给他。

"它不可爱吗?吉姆。我寻遍了全城才找到的,现在你定会一天看数百次了。把你的手表给我,我想看看链子配在它上面会是个什么样子。"

吉姆并没有照她的话去做,却倒在长沙发椅上,双手枕着头,微笑着。

他说:"黛拉,让我们把咱们的圣诞礼物收好暂时保存起来。它们太好了以至于目前无法使用。我把手表卖了拿钱给你买了梳子……。好了,现在咱们吃饭吧。"

Exercises

Part 1 Reading Comprehension

1. Direction: *Decide whether the following statements are true or false according to the text. Write "T" for True and "F" for False.*

1)~5) F F T T F

2. Directions: *Answer the following questions according to the text.*

1) He felt sad or angry.

2) Because Jim managed to have bought the beautiful combs his wife had longed for. And now the wife has cut off her hair.

3) She bought her husband a beautiful watch chain.

4) Open.

Part 2 Words & Structure

1. Directions: *Match an expression in Column B which is similar in meaning to the one in Column A.*

1)~5) c g e j i   6)~10) h b f a d

2. Directions: *Fill in each of the blanks with an appropriate word from the box. Change the form if necessary.*

1) make   2) at   3) instead

4) away   5) longed

Part 3 Translation

1. Directions: *Translate the following passage into Chinese.*

　　因为摆在眼前的是一套梳子——是好几个月来黛拉所羡慕的,摆在一个商店的橱窗里的那套梳子。多么漂亮的梳子,纯玳瑁做的,边上镶着珠宝——颜色恰好配她那秀发。她知道它们是非常昂贵的,对那套梳子她虽然心向神往,但是丝毫没有想过会得到它。而现在它们是她的了,但头发已经卖掉,梳子还有什么用呢。

2. Directions: *Translate the following sentences into English.*

1) The fact is very exaggerating.

2) Once she has resolved on doing it, you won't get her to change her mind.

3) The little girl was very confused by all the noise and activity.

4) I burst into tears when I heard the bad news.

5) She was screaming hysterically because of pain.

Text B

参考译文

战士的最后一封情书

沙利文·巴卢少校

在布尔朗战役(又称马那萨斯战役)开始的一周前,罗德岛第二志愿队的沙利文·巴卢少校给他在史密斯菲尔德家中的妻子写下这封信。

我最亲爱的莎拉:

任务十分紧迫,部队将在数天内开拔,也许就在明天。我觉得有必要写给你几句话,以免今后再没机会给你写信。这样,在我离去的时候,信就会出现在你眼前。

莎拉,我对你的爱永无止境。似乎是有一种结实的锁链将我牢牢系住。但对祖国的热爱似一阵强风,将我和所有这些铁链一起吹向战场。

和你一起度过的所有欢乐时光的记忆如湖水般涌上心头,我为拥有许多那样的日子而感激上帝,感激你。要让我忘掉这些记忆、让我抛却未来的希望是多么难——如果上帝保佑,我们将来能够恩爱地生活在一起,看着咱们的儿子在身边长大成人……

如果我没有回来,我亲爱的莎拉,不要忘记我有多爱你;战场上我即使还剩最后一口气,也会低唤你的名字。原谅我的许多过错和我给你造成的许多伤害。有时候我是多么的愚蠢和没头脑呀。

但是,莎拉!如果故去的人能够重回这个星球,并无声无息、无影无踪地飞绕于他们所爱的人周围,我将在最晴朗的白天和最暗淡的黑夜时时刻刻守候在你的身旁。时时刻刻,直到永远。

当轻柔的风拂过你的脸颊,那将是我的呼吸;当凉爽的风掠过你的鬓角,那将是我路过的灵魂。莎拉,不要为我的死而悲哀:只要想着我走了。等着我,因为我们还会再相逢。

你的：沙利文
1861 年 7 月 14 日
华盛顿特区

Exercises

Part 1　Reading Comprehension

1. Directions：*Decide whether the following statements are true or false according to the text. Write "**T**" for True and "**F**" for False.*

1)～5)　F　T　F　F　F

2. Directions：*Answer the following questions according to the text.*

1) Sullivan Ballou is a major in the Civil War.

2) He wrote to his wife in Smithfield.

3) He wrote this letter before he went to the battlefield.

Part 2　Words & Structure

1. Directions：*Match an expression in **Column B** which is similar in meaning to the one in **Column A**.*

1)～5)　h　c　a　j　i　　　6)～10)　g　b　f　d　e

2. Directions：*Fill in each of the blanks with an appropriate word from the box. Change the form if necessary.*

1) to　　　　　2) with　　　3) indication
4) deathless　　5) resist　　6) over

Part 3　Translation

1. Directions：*Translate the following passage into Chinese.*

　　和你一起度过的所有欢乐时光的记忆如湖水般涌上心头，我为拥有许多那样的日子而感激上帝，感激你。要让我忘掉这些记忆、让我抛却未来的希望是多么难——如果上帝保佑，我们将来能够恩爱地生活在一起，看着咱们的儿子在身边长大成人……

2. Directions：*Translate the following sentences into English.*

1) There is every indication of change in the weather.
2) He volunteered a statement to the police.
3) She said it in a whisper, so I couldn't hear.
4) The old woman still mourns her son's death.
5) The birds flitted about from branch to branch.

Writing Practice

Directions: *For this part, you are allowed 30 minutes to write "**A Letter to Lawrence**", your American friend, to introduce Spring Festival in China and invite him to join you to spend this Spring Festival. Suppose you are Yu Hua. You should write at least 120 words according to the suggestions given below in Chinese.*

Sample

A Letter to Lawrence

December 10, 2006

Dear Lawrence,

It has been five years since we met each other last time. How time flies! How are things with you? The happy time we spent together is always on my mind and I really hope to meet you again. As you know, Spring Festival, Lunar New Year, is the most favorable holiday for us Chinese. With its colorful and rich traditions, it is celebrated almost in every part of China. Everyone is indulged(尽情享受,沉溺于) in the dominant atmosphere of joyous family reunion and with the fresh and vigorous(活力,朝气)look people greet the New Year.

The celebrations vary from place to place, but there are three traditions that have never differed throughout the country. First, the New Year's Eve dinner is a symbol of family reunion, with all family members sitting around the steaming table, tasting a variety of delicious food and wishing each other health, success and happiness. Second, people, during the holidays, will visit each other to express their best regards and wishes. And finally, we can enjoy the marvelous lion and dragon dances symbolizing happiness, good fortune and prosperity.

The day is drawing nearer, my families and I sincerely invite you to join us for this Year's Spring Festival. If you'd like to, we can make further arrangements. Looking forward to your reply!

Yours,

Yu Hua

(230 words)

Further Practice

Part 1　Multiple Choice

Directions: *There are 10 incomplete sentences in this part. For each sentence there are four choices marked **A**, **B**, **C** and **D**. Choose the **ONE** that best completes the sentence*

1~5　B　C　A　C　A　　　　　6~10　D　A　D　A　D

Part 2　Cloze

Directions: *There are 10 blanks in the following passage. For each blank there are four choices marked **A**, **B**, **C** and **D**. Choose the **ONE** that best fits into the passage.*

1~5　C　B　A　B　D　　　　　6~10　C　D　B　A　C
11~15　B　A　C　B　A　　　　16~20　A　D　B　C　C

Part 2　Reading Comprehension

Directions: *Answer the questions after reading the following passage.*

1. No, not many women went down with the ship.
2. Mable Bird, Mrs. Straus's servant, who survived the disaster.
3. Mrs. Straus refused to get into the lifeboat.
4. He was her best friend, her heart's true companion and always a comfort to her soul.
5. Mrs. Straus did not survive for one simple reason: she could not bear to leave her husband.

146

Unit 4 *Economy*

Key & Difficult Points: (重点、难点)

New Words

check, apparently, charge, record, balance, unlikely, error, payment, opportunity, governor, nowadays, superman, broke, percentage, obvious, presently, eliminate, adopt, amass, aspire, bankrupt, bankruptcy, depart, financial, penniless, thirst, wealthy

Phrases & Expressions

ask for, give away, deal with, in the mail, go over, leave out, take care of, all but, for that matter, plow back, let ... pass by, put into effect, after all, draw a blank, cut costs, give in, as good as one's word

Exercises

Listening Practice: Section A (Exercise 1)
Section B (Exercise 2)
Reading Practice: **Text A**   Part 2   Words & Structure (Exercise)
                              Part 3   Translation (Exercise 1)
              Text B   Part 2   Words & Structure (Exercise 2)
                              Part 3   Translation (Exercise 1)
Writing Practice:
Further Practice: Part 1   Multiple Choice
                  Part 2   Cloze
                  Part 3   Reading Comprehension

Listening Practice

Section A

Key to

Exercise 1

Directions: *You will hear 4-5digit numbers. Listen carefully and repeat each number silently after you hear it. Then write it down as quickly as you can.*

1. 7,051   2. 5,231   3. 1,005   4. 4,176   5. 2,500
6. 4,906   7. 13,034   8. 90,372   9. 47,345   10. 67,302

Exercise 2

Directions: *You will hear five sentences. Listen carefully and write down what you hear.*

1. I like Lesson 16 better than Lesson 13.
2. Are there 1,482 students in your school?
3. My address is 121, Market Street.
4. Tom lives at 1,630, 1st Avenue.
5. The 1:50 bus is coming in 14minutes.

Section B

Key to

Exercise 1

Directions: *Listen to the passage and fill in the blanks with the numbers you hear from the recording.*

1. 50   2. 85   3. 175,000   4. 3,000   5. 200,000

Exercise 2

Directions: *Listen to the passage again and choose an appropriate answer for* *each of the following questions.*

1~4　C　B　A　C

Tape-script

For a long time, John Smith had the reputation as a miser. But yesterday, people found they had wronged him.

Mr. Smith was known by other residents as the meanest man in the village. He was a farmer who also owned a building business, and made money on the stock market. A fellow villager, who had known him for more than 50 years, said, "He never spent money on himself. He never bought a new suit and he even mended his shoes with sticky tape rather than buy a new pair."

A woman villager added, "He was the meanest man I ever knew. He got the greatest pleasure from doing his account books. He worked on them for hours. We thought he was planning to take his money with him."

Mr. Smith died in October at the age of 85, and yesterday his will became known. He left $175,000 for the building of houses for his former employees, and $3,000 for a new village bus shelter. The rest of his estate, more than $200,000, went to charity.

Oral Practice

参考译文

对话1

情景

　　每个星期五电视台都要选一位乐于助人的人。两位新闻评论员现在讨论这个"本周人物"。

皮特：　　我们的"每周人物"是珀西·罗斯先生。他的报纸专栏"多谢啦"在200家报纸上都有刊登。罗斯先生就住在梅德维尔。

艾里斯：　是啊，每周给他写信要钱的人多达7000人左右。他读过这些信之后，给其中的一部分人寄钱。他每周还在报纸专栏里给其中三四个人写回信。

皮特： 都有哪些人从罗斯先生那里得到过资助呢？

艾里斯： 通常是老人、病人和贫困儿童。

皮特： 不错。

艾里斯： 有时他不寄钱而是寄给他们所需要的东西。譬如说鞋子、烟火警报器、助听器等。

皮特： 他为什么把钱拿出来资助别人呢？

艾里斯： 他小的时候，家里很穷。他工作很刻苦，现在成为了一名成功的商人。但是罗斯先生没有忘记他幼年时的艰难困苦，他想帮助穷人。

皮特： 他还想在他离开这个人世之前把自己的钱都送给别人，送给那些真正需要钱的人们。

艾里斯： 本周"每周人物"栏目，他是一个不错的人选。

对话 2

情景

费利克斯的支票账户有个问题，他不知道如何解决。于是他来到银行问出纳员。

出纳员： 你好，我能帮助你吗？

费利克斯： 是的。我的支票账户有个问题。

出纳员： 什么问题？

费利克斯： 我在邮件中收到了这个通知，是关于透支的事。

出纳员： 我看一下。……. 显然，你上次开的 59 美元的支票，账上没有足够的款项支付，所以银行将 64 美元记入你账户的借方。这里包括 5 美元银行手续费。

费利克斯： 银行会不会计算错了呢？根据我的记录。账面余额应该有 41 美元。

出纳员： 稍等，我查一下。……没错。根据银行到昨天营业日截止时的记录，你收到的通知是对的。

费利克斯： 奇怪了。我在分行存钱 10 年了，从来没有透支过。

出纳员： 银行不太可能出错的。要不要我再核对一下你的账？

费利克斯： 请再核对一下吧。这是我的付款记录。

出纳员： 好了，余额是欠 59 美元。计算机还是对的。你看，你漏算了这张 8 月 1 日开的 100 美元支票哦。

费利克斯： 哦？让我看一下。……对不起，我总是算不清数字。

出纳员： 没关系。我们有时候都会出错的。

费利克斯： 你说得对。不管怎么说，我现在要在账上存进 300 美元，这样所有问题都解决了。

Reading Practice

Text A

参考译文

如何赚钱？

有些人看到一项投资时便能判定它是一个有利可图的投资，有些人却让宝贵的机会擦肩而过。

就拿彼得·米纽伊特来说，他是新阿姆斯特丹（现在的纽约市）的州长，他用价值相当于 24 美元的工具和布匹从当地的印第安人手中买下了曼哈顿岛。现在的 24 美元在纽约连 1 平方英尺的写字间也买不下来！这点儿钱只够你用来停几个小时的车。

那么，那些于 1938 年因为破产，以 65 美元的价钱把他们连环画主角"超人"的版权卖给了一个出版商的创造者们的情况又是怎么样呢？现在仅《超人》电影一项就能带来数亿美元的收入。

有时一项交易能够使双方都受益。早在 20 世纪 20 年代一个人与一家生产火柴的公司联系。他告诉火柴公司他发现如果在他们的生产过程中稍加变化就能为他们节约很多钱。他担保这个变化实施起来不需任何成本。如果他们实施这个计划的话，他本人只想得到所获节约利润的百分之一。

火柴公司对这个人的提议丝毫不感兴趣。毕竟，如果这项提议连一个普通人都能发现的话，无疑他们自己的研究小组早就已经会发现了。他们于是花了数月时间试图找到减少成本的途径，但是没能成功。最后他们放弃了，并把那个人找来了。他们同意如果真的能够节约开支的话，他就能得到他想要的那 1%。

这个人履行了他的诺言。他是这样对他们说的："你们现在的每个火柴盒上有两个划火的面，但你们实际上只需要一个。如果去掉一个划火的面，你们就能立刻节省开支。"

公司采纳了他的建议，节约了开支，并付给了他该得的那份。你是否也有能够令你成为百万富翁的好主意呢？

Exercises

Part 1　Reading Comprehension

Directions：*Answer the questions according to the text Orally.*

1. He bought the island of Manhattan from the local Indians for 24 dollars' worth of tools and cloth. Nowadays 24 dollars wouldn't buy one square foot of office space in New York! For that price now, you could park your car for a few hours.

2. The creators of Superman sold their rights of the comic strip hero to a publisher for 65 dollars in 1938 because they were broke. Nowadays the Superman movies alone bring hundreds of millions of dollars!

3. Two sides. The man and the match company.

4. The man thought that his discovery could save the match company a lot of money.

5. He wanted one percent of the savings.

6. They thought if the idea was so obvious to an ordinary person, surely their own research team would have come up with it already.

7. They gave in and called the man in.

8. Yes, he did.

9. The match company presently put two striking surfaces on each match box, but they really only needed one. If they eliminated one of the surfaces, they would have instant savings.

10. Yes, they did.

Part 2　Words & Structure

Directions：*Fill in each of the blanks with an appropriate word or phrase from the box. Change the form if necessary.*

1. adopt
2. came up with
3. After all
4. drew a blank
5. as good as his word
6. went ahead with
7. passes by
8. worth of
9. alone
10. give in

Part 3   Translation

1. Directions：*Translate the following sentences into English.*

1) He was broke，and his friends were not willing to lend him any more money.

2) He sold the right of the book to a press.

3) You cannot let any opportunity pass by.

4) He has many bright ideas.

5) He is always as good as his word.

6) We are going to go ahead with this policy next year.

7) The young man came up with a new way to learn English.

8) I really can't understand why you gave in.

9) This project alone cost a million dollars.

10) I asked him for help，but drew a blank.

2. Directions：*Translate the following sentences into Chinese.*

1) 有些人却让机会擦肩而过。

2) 就拿彼得·米纽伊特来说,他是新阿姆斯特丹(现在的纽约市)的州长,他用价值相当于 24 美元的工具和布匹从当地的印第安人手中买下了曼哈顿岛。

3) 那么,那些于 1938 年因为破产,以 65 美元的价钱把他们连环画主角"超人"的版权卖给了一个出版商的创造者们的情况又是怎么样呢?

4) 现在仅《超人》电影一项就能带来数亿美元的收入。

5) 他担保这个变化实施起来不需任何成本。

6) 如果他们实施这个计划的话,他本人只想得到所获节约利润的百分之一。

7) 毕竟,如果这项提议连一个普通人都能发现的话,无疑他们自己的研究小组早就已经发现了。

8) 于是他们花了数月时间试图找到减少成本的途径，但是没能成功。

9) 这个人履行了他的诺言。

10) 如果去掉一个划火的面,你们就能立刻节省开支。

Text B

参考译文

钱只是原材料

在人们一系列的烦恼中,钱几乎总是名列前茅。

一项《华尔街日报》的研究发现百分之七十的公众其工资收入仅够开销,毫无剩余。自 1975 年以来按揭借债了百分之三百,而且消费者破产达到有史以来最高。经济问题被列为导致大多数婚姻失败的一个因素。我们是深受经济压力折磨的人。那么我们到底应该怎样看待金钱呢?

正像《圣经》告诫我们的那样,担心钱或诸如此类的事情不会给我们带来任何好处。耶稣曾经问道:"你们有谁能靠忧虑使自己的生命延长哪怕一个小时?""你们为什么要为衣服烦恼呢? 看见田野里的百合花是怎么生长的吗? 它们从不耕田纺纱。"

尽管我的内心渴望像百合花那样生活。但我的头脑里却感到需要储藏囤积。

能够不受经济困扰而生活的人,或者能够把钱花在别人身上就像花在自己身上那么自在的人,都是不寻常的人。

托马斯·爱迪生就是这种难得的人。如果这位大发明家把他的钱积蓄起来,去世的时候就会是一个大富翁。他第一项成功的发明使他净得四万美元,这在 1869 年是一笔巨款。他一生中获得了 1093 项发明专利,然而,在他离开这个世界时却身无分文。

多年后,他的儿子查尔斯回忆起自己父亲对钱的态度时说:"他把钱看作原材料,就像金属一样,是给人用的,而不是让人聚积的,因此他一直把自己的基金重新投资到新的项目中去。有好几次他将近破产,但他决不让钱主宰他的行动。"

约翰·卫斯礼也一样。这位卫斯礼会的创始人在 18 世纪的英国收入最高,但他把自己的收入都给了别人。他的金钱观很简单:"尽量挣,尽量省,尽量给。"

对我们大多数人来说,不管我们拥有多少钱,总是不够。也许我们应该记住:钱只是一种原材料,要用来投资其他方面的。

Exercises

Part 1 Reading Comprehension

1. **Directions**: *Decide whether the following statements are true or false*

*according to the text. Write "**T**" for True and "**F**" for False.*

1)~5)　T　T　F　T　T

2. Directions：*Discuss the following questions in group.*

1）I agree with this opinion，because if you plow money back into new investments，you will contribute more to society and at the same time you are likely to make more money，which will be put to even better use. This will from a really beneficial service to yourself and others as well. It will thus promote the development of our modern society.

2）I don't agree with this opinion. We make money in order to spend it，so we can get more joy from life. We can buy what we want to buy，such as beautiful clothes，delicious foods，books. If we didn't spend money on the things we like，what's the point of making money? Life would be all but misery and toil if we only know how to make money.

Part 2　Words & Structure

1. Directions：*Read the following pairs of sentences carefully and tell the different meanings of the word in each pair.*

1）A. 为(某种思想/感情)所折磨　　　B. 消耗；消磨

2）A. 繁殖；培植　　　B. 品种

3）A. 不熟练的；无经验的　　　B. 未经加工的

4）A. 重读　　　B. 持续的压力；紧张

5）A. 哲学　　　B. 生活的信念或原则

6）A. 净的　　　B. 网

7）A. 写　　　B. 传递思想

8）A. 使旋转　　　B. 纺纱，纺线

2. Directions：*Fill in each of the blanks with an appropriate phrase from the box. Change the form if necessary.*

1）at the top

2）free from

3）all but

4）do anyone any good

5）rather than

6) adds... to

7) plowed back into

8) gave... away

9) for that matter

Part 3　Translation

1. Directions: *Translate the following passage into Chinese.*

1) 在人们噶系列的烦恼中,钱几乎总是名列前茅。

2) 经济问题被列为导致大多数婚姻失败的一个因素。

3) 尽管我的内心渴望像百合花那样生活,但我的头脑里却感到需要储藏囤积。

4) 能够不受经济困扰而生活的人都是不寻常的人。

5) 钱只是一种原材料,要用来投资其他方面的。

2. Directions: *Translate the following sentences into English.*

1) The students are thirsting for knowledge.

2) The cold medicine tastes nice, but it doesn't do me any good.

3) This lecture is all but three hours.

4) I'd rather go to school on foot rather than by that old bike.

5) My philosophy about life is: be happy everyday.

Writing Practice

Directions: *Write a composition entitled* **"Money and Happiness"** *within at least 120 words.*

Sample

Money and Happiness

Money is very important in our lives. Many people think that when you have money you can be happy. That means if a person is poor, he can never be happy.

In my opinion, money is important for food, clothing, shelter and transportation. Without money, we could have done nothing. But that does not mean that only the rich are happy. Rich people are too busy earning money to enjoy life. They are constantly worrying about losing their fortune. How can they be happy? On the contrary, if a person is penniless, he has to worry about money all the time, so he won't be happy either.

The really happy person is one who has enough money so that he can do whatever he wants. He is not crazy for money and is content with life.

(136 words)

Further Practice

Part 1   Multiple Choice

Directions: *There are 10 incomplete sentences in this part. For each sentence there are four choices marked **A**, **B**, **C** and **D**. Choose the **ONE** that best completes the sentence.*

1~5 A B D A B   6~10 D D A C C

Part 2   Cloze

Directions: *There are 20 blanks in this passage, and for each blank there are four choices marked A, B, C, and D at the end of the passage. You should choose the **ONE** that best fits into the passage.*

1~5 B A C C B   6~10 D A D D A
11~15 B A C B C   16~20 B D C A B

Part 3   Reading Comprehension

Directions: *Read the passage and then tell whether the statements below it are true "T" or false "F".*

1~5 F F T T F

Unit 5 *Health*

Key & Difficult Points：(重点、难点)

New Words

patient, trouble, tongue, scientific, temperature, strange, measure, degree, normal, blood, serious, awful, fever, stomach, prescribe, prescription, advice, daylight, weak, grow, belly, boost, diverse, energize, immune, optimistic, stressful

Phrases & Expressions

be likely to, be tired of, let oneself go, make sense of, put on, rely on

Exercises

Listening Practice：Section A (Exercises 1, 2)
Section B (Exercise 1)
Reading Practice： **Text A**　　Part 2　Words & Structure (Exercise 1)
　　　　　　　　　　　　　　Part 3　Translation(Exercise 3)
　　　　　　　　　Text B　Part 2　Words & Structure(Exercise 2)
　　　　　　　　　　　　　　Part 3　Translation (Exercise 2)
Writing Practice
Further Practice：Part 1　Multiple Choice
　　　　　　　　Part 2　Cloze
　　　　　　　　Part 3　Reading Comprehension

Listening Practice

Section A

Key to

Exercise 1

Directions: *Here are five recorded questions. When you hear each question, you should decide on the correct answer from the 4 choices marked A, B, C and D.*

1~5 C B D B A

Tape-script

1. How is your brother getting along with his study?
2. How do you find our new manager?
3. When are you going to discuss our plan?
4. Which do you prefer, coffee or tea?
5. Hello, can I speak to Mr. Simpson, please?

Exercise 2

Directions: *Here are five recorded dialogues. After each dialogue, there is a recorded question. When you hear a dialogue and a question, you should decide on the correct answer from the 4 choices marked A, B, C and D.*

1~5 A C B A D

Tape-script

1. M: Could you give me a wake-up call tomorrow morning at 5:30?
    W: Certainly. Tell me your room number, please.
    Q: Where does the conversation most probably take place?
2. M: Nancy bought a computer for only $1,500 last week.
    W: Really? I'd like to have a look at it.
    Q: What did Nancy buy?

3. M: How do you feel about the test?

W: There were many difficult questions I couldn't answer.

Q: How did the woman feel about the test?

4. M: What did you do over the weekend?

W: Oh, we had a wonderful time on the beach.

Q: Where did the woman go on the weekend?

5. M: Why, you look so pale! What's wrong with you?

W: I have a terrible headache.

Q: What do we know about the woman?

Section B

Key to

Exercise 1

Directions: *Here's a recorded short passage. The passage is printed out, but some words or phrases missing. You are required to put the missing words or phrases according to what you hear.*

(1) suffering from

(2) however

(3) explained

(4) afraid of

(5) common

Tape-script

Jim is my brother-in-law. He was suffering from a toothache last week. But he didn't want to see a doctor. Finally, however, my mother-in-law decided that she would go and see the doctor herself. She carefully explained that although her son had a lot of pain, he was refusing to get treatment. Her son was afraid of doctors. The nurse told her that they were used to dealing with this common fear and would be able to fit Jim in right away. "How old is your little boy?" she asked. My mother-in-law replied, "He's 40 years old."

Exercise 2

Directions: You will hear a recorded passage. After that you will hear five questions. When you hear a question, you should complete the following incomplete

answer to it with a word or a phrase.

1. grandmother
2. grandmother's house
3. her life
4. forest
5. A few/ Several years

Tape-script

The most important person in my childhood was my grandmother. I really loved going to her house during vacations. She would tell me many stories about her life during World War II. Also, she would tell me interesting stories about people and animals. Sometimes she made up her own stories. We often went into the forest to pick flowers. She taught me which ones to pick and which ones I should avoid because they are poisonous. When I was sad, my grandmother would rock me and sing pretty songs to me. I can still hear her sweet and gentle voice. She died a few years ago, and now I miss her very much.

Questions:

1. Who was the most important person in the speaker's childhood?
2. Where did the speaker like to go during his vacations?
3. What kind of stories did the speaker's grandmother tell him?
4. Where did they sometimes go and pick flowers?
5. When did the speaker's grandmother die?

Oral Practice

参考译文

对话1

情景

> 一个病人感到头痛、肚子也痛，时而觉得热时而觉得冷，所以他来到医院看病。

医生：上午好。我想你是新来的病人。怎么啦？

病人：我感到时冷时热的，还头痛、胃痛的。

医生：哦，你看起来脸色不好。

病人：请问是什么颜色？

医生：对不起，我所说的是"off-color"。这是一个词组，用来描述当人们身体不舒服时的脸色或感觉。来，把体温表放在舌头下（量一下体温），我们尽量更科学一些，什么时候开始这样的？

病人：昨晚睡觉时觉得很累，今天早上醒来就觉着身体很糟糕。

医生：哦，知道了。咱们瞧一下你的体温。和我想的一样，101度。

病人：啊！101度？这么高哇？

医生：是啊，你听起来这好奇怪。我们现在常用华氏温标来计量人们的体温。这样人的正常血液温度为98.4度。如果用摄氏温标的话，你的体温是39度，有点高，但并不是水的沸点。

病人：哦，那么还不太重。

医生：是的，不重。

对话2

情景

> 琳达喉咙痛、头痛。她来找史密斯大夫看病。

史密斯医生：你感觉怎么样？

琳达：　　　太可怕了。喉咙痛，头也痛。

史密斯医生：哦，量一下你的体温看你是否发烧。102度。你确实发烧了。咳嗽吗？

琳达：　　　不咳嗽。

史密斯医生：耳朵痛吗？

琳达：　　　不痛。

史密斯医生：胃痛吗？

琳达：　　　胃不痛。就是喉咙痛、头痛，很难受。

史密斯医生：可能你患上流感了。这病使你感到浑身难受。我来检查一下你的喉咙、听听你的胸部。你的喉咙有点红，但你的胸部听起来没事。你应该卧床休息、多喝水，我给你开一些药。每天服4次，每次一片，共服10天，好吗？

琳达：　　　好吧，谢谢，史密斯医生。

史密斯医生：不用谢。没事，琳达。当你举行婚礼时，你不想生病吧。哦，等一下！别忘了拿你的处方。

Reading Practice

Text A

参考译文

健康习惯

习惯就是我们经常做而且做的时候用不着考虑的事。我们可以有好习惯，也可以有坏习惯。

本文提供一些有关如何保持健康的建议。它告诉你想保持健康必须得做什么，还告诉你不该做什么。它谈到好习惯和坏习惯。

早睡早起使人健康、富有、聪明。

这是个古老的英语俗语。它的意思是说，我们必须早睡，早上必须早起。如果我们这样做了，就能身体健康，还能有钱（富有）、聪明（明智）。

真是这样吗？可能的确如此。需要足够的睡眠。儿童每天需要睡10个小时。如果不早睡就得不到足够的睡眠，那样你就不能很好地思考问题，你就不会变聪明，也不能变得富有了！

有人晚上睡得晚，早上起得晚。这对他们是不好的。晚上天黑了，我们就必须去睡觉。黑暗有助于我们睡得好。白天来临，我们必须起床。该是锻炼的时间了。散步、跑步、跳跃、游泳和打球都是锻炼。如果身体不运动就会变得虚弱。锻炼就能使身体强壮。

锻炼可以帮助血液在身体内循环。血液将养分带到我们身体的各个部位。头部里的大脑也需要血液。我们用大脑思考。如果我们保持身体健康，经常锻炼，就能更好地思考！

另一个对健康非常重要的东西是食物。如果我们想身体健康就必须吃足够的食物。这些食物必须是按正确的方法烹调的干净食物，品种也必须恰当。

米饭和面包对我们都有益。它们帮助我们工作，天冷时让我们暖和。但是如果不吃其他食物，我们就会生病。

肉、鱼、牛奶、水果和蔬菜对我们都很有益。它们帮助我们长身体，让我们保持健康。我们必须每天吃点这些种类的食物。

Exercises

Part 1   Reading Comprehension

1. Directions: *Read the text carefully, and then decide whether the following statements are true or false. Write "T" for true and "F" for false.*

1)~4)   T T F T   5)~8)   F F F T

2. Directions: *Answer the following questions according to the text.*

1) A habit is something people do very often.

2) Going to bed early and getting up early.

3) Yes, because our body must get enough sleep.

4) Ten hours.

5) We cannot think properly.

6) Rice and meat, fruit and vegetables, fish, milk, and eggs.

3. Directions: *Discuss the following questions with your classmates.*
(Omitted)

Part 2   Words & Structure

1. Directions: *There are 10 incomplete sentences in this part. For each sentence*

*there are four choices marked **A**, **B**, **C** and **D**. Choose the answer
that best competes the sentence.*

1)～5)　A B C D D　　　6)～10)　B A C A D

2. Directions：*Match the words on **Column A** with the appropriate definitions in
Column B.*

1)～5)　e i b g h　　　6)～10)　j c d a f

Part 3　Translation

1. Directions：*Translate the following sentences into Chinese*：

1)本文提供一些有关如何保持健康的建议。

2)早睡早起使人健康、富有、聪明。

3) 儿童每天需要睡 10 个小时。

4)锻炼可以帮助血液在身体内循环。

5)血液将养分带到我们身体的各个部位。

2. Directions：*Translate the following sentences into English*：

1) He gave us some good advice.

2) This book gives all kinds of useful information on how to repair cars.

3) Reading aloud is very important in learning English.

4) We usually take the children to school in the car.

5) An example helps show exactly what a word means.

6) My hair has grown too long.

Text B

参考译文

如何保持健康

　　某些身心疗法能帮助我们所有人减少压力、改进人生观从而使你保持健康。
下面就谈几种供我们大家选择：

　　1. 把那些消极的、令人不快的事情写下来。人们写的过程就有助于将事件理
一理,这会使他们更好地了解自己的处境。通过写能使你明白这种紧张的经历是
怎么一回事,你就不会那样去想或担忧了。而当你不那么紧张了,你的免疫功能也

就增强了。至于写多少或写多久,这要取决于事情本身给你带来的紧张程度。建议你最好一直写到不愿写为止,然后读一遍自己所写的东西,这会使你对所写的事情有更多的了解。

2. 与朋友谈论自己经受的压力同样也能起到像上面所谈到的一样积极的作用。

3. 请求家人、朋友和同事们的支持。从他人那里所得到的理解能够减少紧张,从而有利于免疫系统。当有人爱你、关心你,同你分担问题和情感时,你会感到你不是孤身一人在与困难和环境斗争。你的社交面越广泛越好,而且那些有很多不同社会关系的人比那些社会关系少的人得感冒的机会要小。

4. 腹部呼吸法。在一个安静的房间坐在一张舒适的椅子上,闭上眼睛,用鼻子呼吸,让腹部充满空气,然后将气慢慢从嘴里呼出。

5. 慢慢地散步。慢慢地散步的同时时时刻刻注意正在发生的一切——你是否感到有风扑面吹来,有只小虫在你身边飞舞,或者听到小鸟在唱。即使你在思考那些问题,你也会比原先平静些,使问题离你远一些。

6. 跳跳舞。假如你在家里,你可以跳舞。播放一些快节奏的音乐,关上门,让自己纵情地跳。跳舞能给你活力,仅这一点就能使你感觉好一些。

不管哪些身心疗法对你最有效,千万不能依赖它们,不能一味地依赖它们以保持身心健康。正如体育锻炼、良好的营养和适当的医疗保健等一样,都只是保持身体健康良方的一部分。不过它们却是一个重要的组成部分。

Exercises

Part 1　Reading Comprehension

1. **Directions**：*Decide whether the following statements are true or false according to the text. Write "**T**" for True and "**F**" for False.*

1~4　F　T　T　T

2. Directions：*Work in pairs to discuss the following questions.*

Sample

Other mind-body techniques include：

— singing；

— sports；

— fishing；

— talking;

— meditation;

— taiji;

— traveling.

Part 2　Words & Structure

1. Directions：*Read the sentences carefully and choose the **ONE** in which the italicized word has the same meaning as in the sentence quoted from the passage.*

1）A：人生观　　　　　　　B：前景

2）A：依次　　　　　　　　B：反过来

3）A：疲倦　　　　　　　　B：厌烦

4）A：单独地　　　　　　　B：仅仅

5）A：(某种食物的)烹饪法　　B：用于词组"be a recipe for"表示很可能产生某种结果的

6）A：仍然　　　　　　　　B：甚至，更

7）A：调料　　　　　　　　B：达到某种特定目标所需的东西

2. Directions：*Fill in each of the blanks with an appropriate word or phrase from the box. Change the form if necessary.*

1）distance　　　2) reverse　　　3) am likely to　　4) put...on

5）make a sense of 6) let myself go　7) am tired of　　8) boost

Part 3　Translation

1. Directions：*Translate the following sentences into Chinese.*

1）某些身心疗法能帮助我们所有人减少压力、改进人生观从而使你保持健康。

2）人们写的过程就有助于将事件理一理，这会使他们更好地了解自己时处境。

3）从他人那里所得到的理解能够减少紧张，从而有利于免疫系统。

4）当有人爱你、关心你，同你分担问题和情感时，你会感到你不是孤身一人在与困难和环境斗争。

5）你的社交面越广泛越好，而且那些有很多不同社会关系的人比那些社会关系少的人得感冒的机会要小。

6）不管哪些身心疗法对你最有效，千万不能依赖它们，不能一味地依赖它们以保持身心健康。

2. Directions: *Translate the following sentences into English.*

1) We need a vacation to boost our spirits.

2) He did the reverse of what we expected; instead of being angry, he bought us a drink.

3) They can both run equally fast.

4) Our factory started to make many diverse kinds of products.

5) Let go! You're hurting my arm.

6) Whether the game will be played depends on the weather.

7) Take whichever seat you like.

Writing Practice

Directions: *Write a composition entitled "Good Health" with at least than 120 words (Not including the given opening sentence). Your composition should be based on the OUTLINE below and should start with the given opening sentence: "The desire for good health is universal."*

Sample

Good Health

The desire for good health is universal. No matter what we do, we must have sound bodies. Because good health is the foundation for us to fulfill our work.

There are many ways to keep fit. Clear air and water, nutritious food, moderate activity, a little walk in the sunshine, and a good night's sleep; the key here is persistence. Moreover, we should pay attention to spiritual well-being. If we want to improve our health, we must face the life with smiles.

Personally speaking, I watch my diet very much. I try to avoid all processed foods, avoid foods high in fat, salt, and sugar, and concentrate on increasing the amount of fresh fruits and vegetables in the diet. It does a lot of good to my health. Furthermore, I devote part of my time to doing regular physical exercises.

(140 words)

Further Practice

Part 1 Multiple Choice

Directions: *There are 10 incomplete sentences in this part. For each sentence there are four choices marked **A**, **B**, **C** and **D**. Choose the **ONE** that best completes the sentence.*

1~5 D C A C D   6~10 C B D D A

Part 2 Cloze

Directions: *There are 20 blanks in this passage, and for each blank there are four choices marked A, B, C, and D at the end of the passage. You should choose the **ONE** that best fits into the passage.*

  1~5 D C B C D   6~10 A D A B B
11~15 C B A C A   16~20 C B A C C

Part 3 Reading Comprehension

Directions: *Choose the best answer after reading the following passage.*

1~5 A D B D D

Key & Difficult Points : (重点、难点)

New Words

definitely, stylish, tropical, welfare, incredible, average, burglar, unwanted, pest, topic, property, race, train, breed, retired, fancier, keep, royal, bite, reserved

Phrases & Expressions

switch on, control screen, pick out, never mind, call the roll, treat... as..., have an eye for, provide with, interact with, protect from

Exercises

Listening Practice: Section B (Exercise 1, 2)
Reading Practice: **Text A**   Part 2   Words & Structure (Exercises 1, 2)
                              Part 3   Translation (Exercise 2)
                Text B   Part 2   Words & Structure (Exercises 1, 2)
                              Part 3   Translation (Exercise 2)
Writing Practice
Further Practice: Part 1   Multiple Choice

Listening Practice

Section A

Key to

Exercise 1

Directions: *In this section, you will hear a song. Listen to the song carefully and fill in the blanks with the exact words you have just heard.*

(1) hope   (2) take   (3) alone   (4) have

(5) paper   (6) robbers   (7) shine   (8) protect

(9) scare   (10) bunny   (11) talks   (12) goldfish

Tape-script

How Much Is the Doggie in the Window

How much is that doggie in the window? (arf! arf!)

The one with the waggly tail.

How much is that doggie in the window? (arf! arf!)

I do hope that doggie's for sale.

I must take a trip to California.

And leave my poor sweetheart alone.

If he has a dog, he won't be lonesome.

And the doggie will have a good home.

How much is that doggie in the window? (arf! arf!)

The one with the waggly tail.

How much is that doggie in the window? (arf! arf!)

I do hope that doggie's for sale.

I read in the paper there are robbers. (roof! roof!)

With flashlights that shine in the dark.

My love needs a doggie to protect him.

And scare them away with one bark.

I don't want a bunny or a kitty.

I don't want a parrot that talks.
I don't want a bowl of little fishes.
He can't take a goldfish for a walk.
How much is that doggie in the window? (arf! arf!)
The one with the waggly tail.
How much is that doggie in the window? (arf! arf!)
I do hope that doggie's for sale.

Section B

Key to

Exercise 1

Directions: *Listen to the story and choose the best answer to each question you hear.*

1~5 D B D C C

Exercise 2

Directions: *Listen to the story again and write down your answer to each of the following questions.*

1. He often asked Blackie to amuse his friends with some tricks.
2. Because he wanted to send Blackie for some cough syrup.
3. More than half an hour.
4. Less than five dollars.
5. Blackie might have spent it on a bone.

Tape-script

Ramon Was Proud of Blackie

Ramon was very proud of his dog Blackie. Whenever he got the chance, he would ask his dog to amuse his friends with some tricks.

One day Ramon went to visit his friend Frank who was sick at home with a bad cold. "How are you feeling?" asked Ramon. "Worse than yesterday," replied

Frank, "I have a terrible cough, and there's not a drop of medicine in the house."

"Cheer up, Frank. I'll send Blackie to the local drugstore for some cough syrup. He'll be back in a minute, before you know it." Ramon put a five-dollar note in Blackie's mouth and the dog ran down the street. "And keep the change," Ramon shouted after him.

"Oh, Ramon, don't be silly. You know that dog won't be back with any medicine." "Oh yes, he will," replied Ramon. Half an hour later, however, Blackie had not returned. Ramon was feeling embarrassed, and felt angry at his friend's little smile.

"Something has happened to him, I'm sure." said Ramon, "He obeyed me as a rule." Just then Frank saw Blackie at a distance. He hurried to open the door and let him in. Frank was shocked to see a bottle of medicine in the dog's mouth.

"Good boy," said Ramon, "But what took you so long?" Blackie ran over to the window, barking and wagging his tail. Ramon glanced out and saw a bone outside.

Oral Practice

参考译文

对话 1

> **情景**
> 　　王龙是一名新入学的学生。今天他要在语言实验室上他的第一次听力课。下面是他与刘教授之间的对话。

王　龙：刘教授,早上好。
刘教授：王龙,早上好。
王　龙：我能进来吗?
刘教授：当然可以。你能否在外面换上拖鞋进来?
王　龙：对不起,我不知道。我保证以后不再这样做。
刘教授：王龙,你知道如何使用语言实验室的机器吗?

王　龙：不知道。这是我在这里上的第一堂英语课。

刘教授：请打开开关，然后我的控制台上就记录你的出勤，你明白了吗？

王　龙：我明白了。在听的时候能用我的磁带吗？

刘教授：当然不能。

王　龙：好，我这就取出我的磁带，戴上耳机。

刘教授：顺便说一句，如果你发现声音不太合适的话，只须调节一下音量键。

王　龙：谢谢你的帮助。

刘教授：没关系。

对话 2

情景

听力课开始了。刘教授正在告诉学生们怎么做。下面是王龙与刘教授之间的对话。

王　龙：(打开呼叫键)老师，我能打扰一下您吗？

刘教授：王龙，怎么了？我正在点名。

王　龙：我听不清你说什么。

刘教授：别着急，把声音键调大些，现在能听清楚吗？

王　龙：好多了，你能重复一下刚才说的吗？

刘教授：请翻到第五页，看第二单元。

王　龙：噢，谢谢。

刘教授：不要把麦克风离你的嘴太近，否则会有杂音。

王　龙：我明白了，现在可以吗？

刘教授：可以。

王　龙：很抱歉打扰您了。

刘教授：注意，磁带录音开始了，快跟上。

Reading Practice

Text A

参考译文

美国人眼中的宠物

　　美国人喜爱宠物,而且并非是一时之爱。很多宠物的主人把宠物当作是家庭的一部分,有时他们会给宠物一些有趣的录像带和玩具。如果宠物的主人对时尚很有鉴赏力的话,他们就会给他们的宠物穿上漂亮的衣裳。你也许会说美国人对待他们的宠物就像对待他们的孩子一样——有时甚至会更好。

　　在美国,拥有宠物的家庭多于拥有孩子的家庭。至少有43%的美国家庭饲养着某种宠物。一些动物,如猴子,蛇,甚至于狼,都可以住在美国人的家中。更普通的宠物是热带鱼,鼠和鸟。但是猫和狗是美国人最喜欢的宠物。他们认为宠物有权利得到很好的照料,因此美国至少有75家动物福利组织。人们为动物提供了令人难以置信的医疗保健——而且是难以置信的就医价格。人们为他们的宠物买健康保险,轮到和他们的宠物永别的时候,主人们通常会很体面地埋葬宠物。

　　普通的美国人喜欢身边有宠物相伴。研究者发现和动物交流可以降低人的血压。狗能保护主人不受窃贼和不速之客的侵扰,猫能消灭害虫,各种形状和大小的小宠物不仅可以陪伴人们,而且还能给人们带来爱。在很多情况下,饲养宠物能让年轻的夫妇培养起为人父母的责任感。宠物甚至可以促进社会关系。它们可以使主人友善,还为人们交谈提供了一个很好的话题。

　　如同热狗或苹果馅饼一样,宠物是美国文化的一个基本组成部分。对美国人来说,宠物不仅仅是财产,而且也是家庭的一部分。毕竟,宠物也是有情有义的生命体。

Exercises

Part 1　Reading Comprehension

Directions: *Choose the best answer according to the text.*

1~6　C　D　B　D　A　C

Part 2　Words & Structure

1. Directions: *Match an expression in* **Column B** *which is similar in meaning to the* **ONE** *in Column A.*

1)~5)　c　e　d　i　j　　　　6)~10)　f　b　h　g　a

2. Directions: *Fill in each of the blanks with an appropriate word or phrase* *from the box. Change the form if necessary.*

1) average   2) encouragement

3) basically   4) be lowered

5) cultured   6) either

7) get rid of   8) believe

9) respectful   10) offered

Part 3   Translation

1. Directions: *Translate the following passage into Chinese.*

宠物不仅仅是我们的伙伴,它们还能使我们学会爱与被爱。很多宠物的主人感到他们的宠物能理解他们,这是因为动物能很快感觉到愤怒和悲伤。在人类的话言不起作用时,猫或狗通常会安慰我们,当宠物因为家、食物、饮料的缘故而依赖我们的时候,我们也会有被爱的感觉。特别是狗,非常尊重主人,这使主人感觉到自己的重要和被需要。

2. Directions: *Translate the following sentences into English.*

1) Jenny treats her pupils like her children.

2) Many students enjoy asking questions in English.

3) They were told that there would be a basketball match the following day.

4) If you do have an eye for fashion, it is time for you to give us an introduction.

5) Sometimes, the West Lake is more beautiful than what we imagine.

6) To tell the truth, she did it awfully. After all, she is your sister.

Text B

参考译文

钟爱动物

英国人十分钟爱动物。他们参加动物比赛,捕捉动物,训练动物并喂养动物。他们喜欢从电视新闻节目中收听有关动物的故事,他们还喜欢读有关动物的书籍。

很多家庭都养宠物,宠物可以是狗、猫或金鱼。一些孤独的老人们喜欢他们的猫或狗就如同喜欢他们的人类朋友一样。当动物爱好者们去世时,他们把钱留给"猫收养所",或"狗收养所",或者是留在"已经退役的马收养所"。

　　动物比赛是另一项非常受欢迎的活动。有些被称为玩赏鸽子的人参加鸽子比赛。他们在自家的花园或阳台上饲养鸽子并训练它们飞回家。要想赛鸽子你不必很有钱,但要想赛马情形就不同了。只有那些有钱人才养得起马并参加赛马。在重大的赛事上,能够看见赛马的主人们身着最漂亮的服装同女王及皇室的其他成员们坐在一起。实际上,真正去看赛马的人不多。但是几乎所有的人在赛马时都下得起赌注,事实上很多人也这样做。无论你在英国的什么地方,你都能在离你不远的地方找到一个赛马赌注登记处。

　　照顾和善待动物只是对动物狂热的表现的一个方面。捕获和杀害动物是英国人的另一大嗜好。例如钓鱼在乡下就是一项最受欢迎的体育运动。数以百万计的人们喜欢在星期六和星期日静静地坐在湖边或河边等待着鱼咬钩。另外还有一些人依然热衷于捕猎狐狸,或射杀鹿或捕获兔子。

　　英国人为什么如此热衷于动物呢? 也许是因为他们与人打交道时过于腼腆和含蓄。"是这样,"一位老妇人这样说道,"我对我的猫说什么都可以,但它从来不会把我看成是傻瓜。"

Exercises

Part 1　Reading Comprehension

Directions: *Please answer the following questions according to the text.*

1. They race them, catch them, train them and breed them.
2. It could be a dog, a cat, or a goldfish.
3. Because they are lonely.
4. Racing pigeons is more common, because only the very rich can afford to keep and race horses.
5. They are seen in their best clothes.
6. They are the Queen and the other members of the Royal Family.
7. They can afford to bet some money on the winners.
8. Whenever you are in Britain, you'll find a "betting shop" not very far away.
9. They catch and kill them. For example, they enjoy fishing, hunting foxes, or shooting deer, or catching rabbits.
10. I can say anything I like to my cat, but she never thinks I'm silly.

Part 2　Words & Structure

1. Directions: *Match an expression in **Column B** which is similar in meaning to* *the ONE in Column A.*

1)~5) c f i j h   6)~10) g b e a d

2. Directions: *Fill in each of the blanks with an appropriate word or phrase*
from the box. Change the form if necessary.

1) breed   2) are crazy about

3) afford   4) were in their best clothes

5) reserved，is different with   6) waiting for，to help

7) bet on   8) hobbies

9) race   10) fancier

Part 3 Translation

1. Directions: *Translate the following passage into Chinese.*

　　对于不同家庭的成员来说,宠物扮演的角色是不同的。对于母亲来说,它们是孩子;对于独生子女来说,它们是兄妹;对于老人来说,它们是孙儿;对我们每个人来说,宠物给我们带来了欢乐,使我们有了更多的伙伴。有人建议把小宠物带上宇宙飞船以陪伴宇航员,帮助他们减少飞行中的压力和孤独。

2. Directions: *Translate the following sentences into English.*

1) That dog bit him in the leg.

2) We should train children to good habits.

3) They breed fish in the reservoir.

4) He is a retired Civil Servant.

5) I live all alone, but I never feel lonely.

Writing Practice

Directions: *This part is to test your ability to do practical writing. You are*
*required to write **a letter of recommendation**, You can write it*
according to the information given below.

Sample

June 20，2006

Dear Sir,

Mr. Li has been employed by this company since July 1999. He was assigned for the responsibility of production control and cost analysis during his service here. He succeeded in incorporating his professional knowledge and good communication skills into his task. Appropriate and insightful proposals were thus made through his effort.

In my opinion, Mr. Li is a motivated and ambitious young man with well-defined goals. He is mature, calm, thoughtful and capable. I am sure he is qualified for advanced scholastic pursuit. I don't hesitate to recommend him to your graduate school.

Sincerely yours,

Chen Fang

Director of the Personnel Department

Feida Industrial Co. Ltd.

(111words)

Further Practice

Part 1　Multiple Choice

Directions: *There are 10 incomplete sentences in this part. For each sentence there are four choices marked A, B, C and D. Choose the ONE that best completes the sentence.*

1~5　D　C　A　D　D　　　　6~10　A　C　C　A　D

Part 2　Cloze

Directions: *Fill in the blanks with the proper words.*

1. largest　　2. weigh　　3. from　　4. for　　5. take
6. like　　7. kill　　8. that　　9. of　　10. other

Part 3　Reading Comprehension

Directions: *Choose the best answer after reading the following passage.*

1~5　A　D　D　C　D

Unit 7 *Happiness*

Key & Difficult Points：(重点、难点)

New Words

flavour, slice, pound, overlook, seemingly, insignificant, chat, succeed, self-conscious, chase, perceive, productive, resilience, surround, heartily, unexpected, incongruous, ridiculous

Phrases & Expressions

propose a toast to one's health, drink a toast to the success, define. . . as. . . , add up, cheer up, equate. . . with. . . , cope with, build up, play with, in the midst of,

Exercises

Listening Practice：Section B(Exercise 1，2)
Reading Practice：**Text A**　Part 2　Words & Structure (Exercises 1，2)
　　　　　　　　　　　　Part 3　Translation (Exercise 2)
　　　　　　　　Text B　Part 2　Words & Structure (Exercise 1，2)
　　　　　　　　　　　　Part 3　Translation (Exercise 2)
Writing Practice
Further Practice：Part 1　Multiple Choice
　　　　　　　　Part 2　Cloze

Listening Practice

Section A

Key to

Exercise 1

Directions: *In this section, you will hear a song. Listen to the song carefully and fill in the blanks with the exact words you have just heard.*

(1) just   (2) pretty   (3) grew   (4) fell   (5) sweetheart

(6) lies   (7) rainbows   (8) own   (9) handsome   (10) tenderly

Tape-script

Que sera, sera

When I was just a little girl,

I asked my mother,

"What will I be?

Will I be pretty?

Will I be rich?"

Here's what she said to me:

"Que sera, sera,

Whatever will be, will be;

The future's not ours to see.

Que sera, sera,

What will be, will be."

When I grew up and fell in love.

I asked my sweetheart,

"What lies ahead?

Will we have rainbows.

Day after day?"

Here's what my sweetheart said:

"Que sera, sera,

Whatever will be, will be;

The future's not ours to see.

Que sera, sera,

What will be, will be. "

Now I have Children of my own.

They ask their mother,

"What will I be?

Will I be handsome?

Will I be rich?"

I tell them tenderly:

"Que sera, sera,

Whatever will be, will be;

The future's not ours to see.

Que sera, sera,

What will be, will be.

Que sera, sera. "

Section B

Key to

Exercise 1

Directions: *Listen to the passage and choose the best answer.*

1~5 C B A C D

Exercise 2

Directions: *Listen to the passage again and fill in the blanks.*

1. funny noses, put on a happy face, put on a sad face, wear funny clothes

2. jump, turn, ride donkeys, push each other, shout, sing

Tape-script

Clowns Are Fun

Clowns like to make people laugh. They paint their faces and put on funny noses. Sometimes they put on a sad face but most of the time they put on a happy face. They also wear funny clothes.

Most clowns work in circuses. They do all kinds of silly things to make the audience laugh. They run, jump, fall down, turn somersaults, and roll over. They ride donkeys backwards. They push each other in wagons or wheelbarrows. Sometimes they shout and sing. Clowns are funny men (and women, too)! A circus is not a circus without clowns!

Children especially enjoy watching clowns. A clown named Cookie often visits hospitals to entertain sick children as well as older people. Sick people need to laugh. It helps them get better faster.

There is an old saying: "Laughter is good medicine."

Oral Practice

参考译文

对话 1

> **情景**
> 江闵先生是中国轻工业品进出口公司的总经理。戈登先生是他的商业合作伙伴。江闵先生为戈登先生举办了晚宴。下面是他们之间的对话:

秘书:请这边走。戈登先生,我们的总经理正在等你。这是江闵先生,中国轻工业品进出口公司的总经理。

戈登:江先生,你好,很高兴有机会能见到你。

江闵:戈登先生,你好。欢迎光临我们的晚宴。旅途顺利吧?

戈登:很好,很顺利。谢谢。

江闵:请坐。

戈登:非常感谢你们为我准备了这么丰盛的晚宴。

江闵:十分荣幸。你喝点什么,茅台还是威士忌?

戈登:茅台是烈性酒,是吗?

江闵:是的,但它是中国最好的酒。你想尝一尝吗?

戈登：好的，我喝一点。

江闵：我提议为你的健康干杯。

戈登：谢谢。我提议为我们合作的良好开端干杯。

合：干杯！

对话 2

情景

　　江闵先生邀请他的另一个商业伙伴约翰逊先生，共进晚餐。下面是他们之间的对话：

江闵：　约翰逊先生，请坐这儿。今天你会品尝到典型的中国菜。

约翰森：这些菜看上去真不错。我的朋友告诉我中国食品很好吃。我很高兴今天有机会尝一尝。

江闵：现在让我们为我们合作成功干一杯。干杯。

约翰森：干杯。

江闵：约翰逊先生，你会用筷子吗？

约翰森：我以前从未用过。但是我想试试。

江闵：很容易。我们中国人通常是这样用的。

约翰森：让我试试。噢，这看上去容易实际上却很难。我恐怕得用刀叉了。

江闵：约翰逊先生，这几个菜是典型的川菜，它们以独特的风味闻名。请吃点蒜泥白肉。

约翰森：谢谢。噢，真好吃，真合我口味。

江闵：热菜来了。我为你夹点怪味鸡片好吗？你会觉得它又辣又咸又甜又酸。

约翰森：谢谢。噢，味道好极了。

江闵：约翰逊先生，请别客气。再吃点烤鸭或其他你喜欢的菜。

约翰森：这些菜都很可口，但是我恐怕不能再吃了。

江闵：请再吃一点点。

约翰森：不能再吃了，谢谢。谢谢你们的热情款待。

江闵：我很高兴你吃得开心。

Reading Practice

Text A

参考译文

幸福是什么

　　我的字典把幸福定义为"幸运"或"好运"。但是我想幸福更好的定义是"享受的能力"。我们越能享受所拥有的一切，我们就越幸福。我们很容易忽视我们从爱与被爱、从交友、从选择居住地的自由、甚至从身体健康中而获得的快乐。

　　我总结了一下我昨天的幸福时刻。首先是我合上最后的饭盒，独自一人在家时的那种无比的幸福。然后是我喜欢的整个上午没有打扰的写作。等到孩子们回家之后，我喜欢在安静的一天过后孩子们吵闹的声音。随后，安静又一次降临。丈夫和我享受着另一种快乐——相依相偎。有时仅仅知道他需要我这件事就使我很幸福。

　　你永远无法知道下一个幸福何时来临。当我问朋友们什么能使他们感到幸福时，他们说的幸福听起来似乎都很平常。"我不喜欢购物"，一位朋友说，"但那里有一个售货员总爱聊天，确实让我很愉快。"

　　还有一位朋友喜欢接电话。"每次电话铃响，我就知道有人正想我呢。"

　　开车也会使我激动。一天我停下来等一辆校车转到路边上，司机冲我咧嘴笑笑，竖起大拇指称赞。在这个疯狂驾车的世界上，我们俩人可谓同盟军了。这使我很高兴。

　　我们都经历过类似的事情，但以之为幸福的人寥寥无几。

　　要想幸福，就需要有愉快的闲暇和满意的工作。我的曾祖母养育了 14 个儿女，还要替人洗衣服，我很怀疑两者中她是否享有其中一个。但她确实有许多亲密的朋友以及家庭，也许正是这些令她很满足。如果她对所拥有的一切很满足，那么也许是因为她没有想到生活可以有另一种完全不同的活法。

　　另一方面，由于我们拥有许多选择且要在各个领域承受争取成功的压力，我们已把幸福变成了另一件我们"必须"拥有的事情。我们因太在意对幸福的"权利"而感到非常痛苦。于是，我们追求（所谓的）"幸福"，将之与"富有"和"成功"等同起来，而没有注意到富有的人、成功的人未必就比普通人幸福。

　　对我们来说，尽管幸福或许并不简单，但要获得幸福，方法却跟从前一样，并不复杂。幸福不在于我们遇到什么事情——而在于我们如何对待所遇到的事情。幸福是从消极因素中寻求积极因素、将挫折视为挑战的能力。幸福不是企盼我们没有的东西,而是满足于享受我们已有的东西。

Exercises

Part 1　Reading Comprehension

Directions: *Please answer the following questions according to the text.*

1. The dictionary defines happy as "lucky" or "fortunate".

2. The author thinks that a better definition of happiness is "the capacity for enjoyment".

3. It's easy to overlook the pleasure we get from loving and being loved, the company of friends, the freedom to live where we please, even good health.

4. No, we can never know where happiness will turn up next.

5. To be happy, we must have enjoyable leisure time and satisfying work.

6. Open. Student's own answer.

7. We have turned happiness into one more thing we "gotta have". It is because we have so many choices and such pressure to succeed in every area.

8. We equate happiness with wealth and success.

9. Happiness isn't about what happens to us—it's about how we perceive what happens to us.

10. We should have the ability of finding a positive for every negative, and viewing a setback as a challenge.

Part 2　Words & Structure

1. Directions: *Match an expression in **Column B** which is similar in meaning to the **ONE** in **Column A**.*

1)~5)　h　g　d　b　c　　　6)~10)　j　e　i　f　a

2. Directions: *Fill in each of the blanks with an appropriate word or phrase from the box. Change the form if necessary.*

1) overlooks	2) fulfill	3) the same	4) viewed as
5) chat	6) chasing	7) cheering up/to be cheered up	
8) seemingly	9) insignificant	10) perceived	

Part 3   Translation

1. Directions: *Translate the following passage into Chinese*.

当我们考虑幸福的时候,我们通常想到一些寻常的事情和最为愉快的时刻,而这种时刻随着年龄的增长越来越少。

对于孩子来说,幸福充满了魔力。我记得在新割下的草堆里捉迷藏;在树林里扮演警察和强盗;在学校演剧中担当有台词的演员。当然孩子也有感到不幸福的时候。但是当他们因赢了赛跑或得了一辆新自行车时而流露出的极度兴奋是没有任何掩饰的。

2. Directions: *Translate the following sentences into English*.

1) You are fortunate to be able to live in this country.

2) Please don't interrupt me when I am talking.

3) The thesis will fulfill the requirements for your M. A.

4) The library has been chasing me for the books.

5) She possessed a beautiful voice.

6) I overlooked the problem and I have to solve it now.

7) The more they talked, the more excited they got.

Text B

参考译文

你在工作中找到乐趣了吗?

根据专家们的看法,工作中缺少幽默确是一种憾事。研究表明,心情愉快的人工作成果大,能产生更多的效益。

现今工作场所里常有的压力是因为不开玩笑。如果你学会了逗笑,那么你和周围的人都会更好地承受压力的风暴。

专家们说,良好的幽默感会有助于你在以下几方面获得成功:

1. 适应变动。现今工作中角色和责任在迅速地变换。幽默感能为你提供应付这种变换所需的韧劲。

2. 提高领导水平。随着事业的发展,可能会让你在机构中承担更多的领导责任,做出更多的决定。培养幽默感会使你具有更有成效的领导能力。

3. 应付加大的压力。如前面所提到的,压力伴随着所有的工作。你承担的责任越大,你经受的压力就越大。而幽默是应付周围压力的一个强有力的工具。欢笑声能帮你消除肌肉紧张,缓解愤怒,增强你克服恐惧及控制忧虑的能力,使你保持一种更为积极的心态。

4. 加强改革和创新的能力。良好的幽默感能提高你创造性思维的能力。

5. 提高交际技能。你机构中的每一个成员都需要有这些技能。幽默既能使他人对你所说的内容更加感兴趣,同时还能有助你被单位他人所接受。

好了,你已经准备好要开怀大笑并且鼓励你的同事们也大笑吗? 以下建议有助于你逐渐学会幽默起来:

第一步:为自己创造幽默的环境,并培养自己的幽默感。怎么做呢? 多看喜剧电影;从杂志和报纸上寻找卡通画看;多与你最风趣的朋友和同事在一起。

第二步:要多开玩笑,不要太严肃。多花点时间陪你的孩子玩,把你认为风趣的事情拟出一张表,每天做一件。

第三步:要经常开心大笑,学会讲笑话。

第四步:玩一些有关语言、双关语及其他用词方面的游戏。

第五步:在日常生活中寻找幽默。寻找生活中意想不到的、不协调的、稀奇古怪和可笑的东西。

第六步:不要和自己过不去,要学会对自己的错误不以为然。

第七步:在压力中寻找幽默。

Exercises

Part 1　Reading Comprehension

Directions: *Decide whether the following statements are true or false according to the text. Write "**T**" for True and "**F**" for False.*

1~5　T　T　F　F　T　　6~10　T　T　F　T　T

Part 2　Words & Structure

1. Directions: *Match an expression in **Column B** which is similar in meaning to the **ONE** in Column A.*

1)~5)　f　h　d　c　e　　　　6)~10)　g　b　i　a　j

2. Directions: *Fill in each of the blanks with an appropriate word from the box. Change the form if necessary.*

1）responsible　　　　　2）positive

3）laughter　　　　　　4）manage

5）decide　　　　　　　6）humor

7）ridiculous　　　　　8）angry

9）increasingly　　　　10）power

Part 3　Translation

1. Directions：*Translate the following passage into Chinese.*

到了少年时期,幸福观发生了变化。突然幸福有了条件,诸如刺激、爱情、名气以及舞会前青春痘是否能消除等。我还能感到因几乎所有的人都被邀请去参加晚会而我未被邀请时的痛苦。我还记得在另一个活动中因与一位和约翰·特拉沃尔塔酷似的人跳舞而出名时的那份激动的心情。

成年时,带来内心欢乐的事情,如出生、爱情和婚姻,也同时带来了责任和失去的危险。对于成年人来说,幸福是复杂的。

2. Directions：*Translate the following sentences into English.*

1）What a shame you didn't win.

2）He was brave and he weathered three crises during his life.

3）Her natural resilience helped her overcome the crisis.

4）This little girl has a good sense of humor.

5）You look ridiculous in those tight jeans.

Writing Practice

Directions：*This part is to test your ability to do practical writing. You are required to write **a letter of Apologies** to the teacher, You can write it according to the information given below.*

Sample

Dear Sir,

I am very sorry that I was unable to go to the school this morning owing to my heart disease. I enclose a certificate from the doctor who is attending me, and he fears it will be several days before I can recover my health.

I trust that my enforced absence will not trouble you any serious inconvenience.

With renewed regrets, I ask to remain.

Yours respectfully,

Zhang Ming

(71words)

Further Practice

Part 1   Multiple Choice

Directions: *There are 10 incomplete sentences in this part. For each sentence there are four choices marked **A**, **B**, **C** and **D**. Choose the **ONE** that best completes the sentence.*

1~5　D　A　C　B　C   6~10　A　B　B　D　B

Part 2   Cloze

Directions: *Fill in the blanks with the proper words.*

1. as   2. from   3. what   4. that   5. be
6. than   7. for   8. than   9. in   10. neither

Part 3   Reading Comprehension

Directions: *Choose the best answer after reading the following passage.*

1~8　B　C　D　D　A　B　C　C

Unit 8 *Science*

Key & Difficult Points: (重点、难点)

New Words

size, hospital, catch, frequently, center, discover, practical, century, power, failure, grope, hesitate, traffic, silent, energy, industry, communication, transmit, distance, property, convenient, circuit, escape, completely, powerful, fix

Phrases & Expressions

go well with, on one's way to, traffic lights, turn off, go through, turn... into, power station, catch fire, jet engine, not... until...

Exercises

Listening Practice: Section A (Exercise 2)
                Section B (Exercise)
Reading Practice: **Text A**   Part 2   Words & Structure (Exercises 1, 2)
                      Part 3   Translation (Exercise)
          Text B   Part 2   Words & Structure (Exercise)
                      Part 3   Translation (Exercise)
Writing Practice
Further Practice: Part 1   Multiple Choice
               Part 2   Cloze

Listening Practice

Section A

Key to

Exercise 1

Directions: *Listen to a passage and decide whether the following statements are true or false. Write "T" for True and "F" for False.*

1~5 F F F T F

Tape-script

My husband and I don't like the schools in our area. We don't think the teachers are very good, and the children don't learn very much. Some children at these schools can't read, it's terrible. Go to the schools and look: the children fight; some of them even smoke and drink. No, our children can have a better education at home with us. After all, we are both teachers.

Exercise 2

Directions: *In this section, you will hear 10 short conversations. At the end of each conversation, a question will be asked about what was said. Listen carefully and choose the best answer.*

1~5 D C A C B   6~10 C C D A B

Tape-script

1. M: Where can I find Helen?

   W: Why not ask John?

   Q: What does the woman mean?

2. M: Excuse me, when will the 8:00 plane arrive?

   W: It's been delayed two hours because of a heavy storm.

   Q: What do we learn from the passage?

3. M: My cousin will be here on Wednesday.

   W: That's the day after tomorrow.

   Q: What day is it today?

4. M: Yesterday I went to Helen's house to listen to records.

    W: I heard she had more than a hundred jazz records. Is that true?

    Q: What do we learn about Helen?

5. W: Are you going to study late again tonight?

    M: I will go to bed early for a change.

    Q: What will the man probably do?

6. W: We can all go swimming at the park after the game.

    M: If it's a nice day, of course.

    Q: What does the man mean?

7. W: These boxes are too heavy for me to move.

    M: Here, I gave you a hand with them.

    Q: What does the man do about these boxes?

8. M: Linda, did you take the empty bottles back to the store?

    W: I got Jack do it.

    Q: What happened to the bottles?

9. M: How about going to the movies after dinner, Mary?

    W: Well, I'll go if you really want to, but I'm a little tired.

    Q: What can you learn from the passage?

10. M: I wonder if I could borrow your car?

    W: You certainly could if I had one.

    Q: What does the woman mean?

Section B

Key to

Exercise

Directions: *Listen to a passage and choose the best answer.*

1~4 C D A A

Tape-script

In the early 1800's, a new kind of power changed transportation and trade along the Mississippi River. This power was steam. People already knew how to use steam engines to run machines. Some people wanted to move boats in the same way. The first steamboat to travel on the Mississippi was the "New Orleans". It made its first trip in 1811. It was a great success, and by 1819 there were 191 steamboats traveling on the river.

In the past the farmers whose products went to other parts of the country used the steamboats. The manufacturers also used the steamboats, whose trade depended on cheap and easy transportation. Today many tourists come to travel on steamboats.

Oral Practice

参考译文

对话1

情景

　　一位客人来到商店,他想买顶帽子,但又不知道该买什么颜色和尺寸的。售货员过来帮他。下面是他们的对话:

顾　客:请问我能看一下那顶帽子吗?

售货员:您需要哪个号的呢?

顾　客:抱歉,这个我不知道。

售货员:让我看一下……您拿六号的吧,您喜欢什么颜色的呢?

顾　客:褐色的吧。

售货员:这些都是褐色的,请您试试这顶吧,很不错的。

顾　客:好的,我来试试。和我的大衣很搭配呢,多少钱?

售货员:九块九毛五,需要我帮您放在盒子里吗?

顾　客:好的,太谢谢你了。

售货员:不用客气。

对话 2

> 海伦是简和大卫的朋友,现在海伦因病住进了医院。今天简没课,她打算去医院看望海伦。在学校门口她遇见了大卫,问他去医院怎么走。

大卫:去哪里呢,简?

简: 我正要去医院看海伦呢。

大卫:我昨天看过她了,她好点了。

简: 去那儿我是不是必须乘 2 路车呢?

大卫:不,不一定,乘 10 路车也能到。

简: 10 路车更多点,是吧?

大卫:是呀,我昨天就坐的 2 路车,在车站我等了半个小时。

简: 谢谢,大卫,我就坐 10 路了。

大卫:但是 10 路车是从镇中心发车的,你要坐的话还得步行两里。

Reading Practice

Text A

参考译文

电

电是两千年以前发现的,而其实际应用仅仅开始于 19 世纪。现在电已在我们的生活中广泛应用。人们如此习惯了电灯、电波、电视和电话,所以很难想象如果没有这些东西生活会变成什么样。一停电,人们就要在闪烁的烛光中四处摸索;车辆就会瘫痪在路上,因为没有信号灯指引它们;冰箱里的食物也会因为停电而坏掉。

在所有形式的能量中,电最有用。电每天供给我们光、热和电力。工农业中用电力开动机器。电使无线电通讯成为可能。

电为什么使用得这样广泛呢? 这是因为电可以通过电线远距离输送,这是电的一个非常重要的特性,所以电使用方便。用一个开关,你就能容易地把电接通或切断。开关开时,电路闭合,电就通过。开关关时,电路断开,电就通不过。除此之外,电能容易地转变成其他形式的能。例如,用电动机可以把电能转变成机械能,电能在电灯中可以转变成光能。

电是从哪里来的呢? 电是从发电站来的。在热电站里人们燃烧煤或石油来发电。在水电站里人们用落水来发电。现在电也可以在核电站中产生。

Exercises

Part 1　Reading Comprehension

Directions: *Decide whether the following statements are true or false according to the text. Write "T" for True and write "F" for False.*

1~4　F　F　F　T　　　5~8　F　F　F　T

Part 2　Words and Structure

1. Directions: *Translate the following phrases.*

1) transmit over long distances

2) radio communication

3) turn on the switch

4) a power failure

5) be changed into light and heat energy

6) 进行实际应用

7) 发现一种新元素

8) 广泛被使用

9) 交通信号灯

10) 发电站

2. Directions: *Fill the blanks by using the proper forms of the words in the bracket.*

1) is turned　　2) practical　　3) imaginations

4) will be built　　5) convenient　　6) be made

Part 3　Translation

Directions: *Translate the following sentences into English.*

1. It is said that another oilfield was discovered in our country last year.

2. The machines in this factory are run with electricity.

3. Electricity can be easily transmitted from power stations to factories.

4. When the circuit is closed, electricity goes through.

5. This nuclear power station was built three years ago.

Text B

参考译文

飞 行

人类总想像鸟儿一样地飞行。鸟儿能够轻易地飞行是因为它们的身体轻,但是人类的躯体可就重多了。

人类起初是通过气球进入空中的,这些气球是充满气体的大袋子。氢气对于气球来说是一种有用的气体,它比空气轻多了。氦也是一种比空气轻的气体,但是它太昂贵,因此气球通常都是装满氢气的。

由于气球没有发动机来作动力,所以气球不得不顺风飞行。后来人类创造了飞艇,它们是具有发动机的气球,但不是圆的,而是长的,发动机在后面。它们也是被充满氢气,其中一些不幸失火,是由于氢气泄漏后被发动机加热而引燃,几秒钟之后,飞艇就整个燃烧起来。

现在有翼的飞机可以带着人们穿越世界,强有力的发动机载着机器横过天空,一些发动机就像小汽车的一样,但比它们的功率大得多。

还有一种我们称之为喷气式装置的发动机。一位英国工程师发明了这种喷气式发动机。1941 年 5 月,他发明的新发动机安装在一架飞机里,这架飞机飞行得很好。与此同时,德国人也建造了一个喷气式飞机发动机,当然两个国家都没告诉对方。

喷气式发动机马力很大。通常在一架飞机里装有两个、三个或四个已经足够了,但一些大的飞机要装六个。在一个正在运动着的喷气式飞机里,任何一个人都可以感觉到这些发动机的力量。喷气式飞机的速度要比声音的传播速度快(声音一秒钟传播约 1100 英尺,也就是 1 小时传播 760 英里)。一架飞行着的喷气式飞机只有它飞过后我们才可听到噪声。

Exercises

Part 1   Reading Comprehension

Directions: *Choose the best answer according to the text.*

1~5   C   B   A   C   C

Part 2   Words and Structure

Directions: *There are 8 incomplete sentences in this part. For each sentence there are four choices marked **A**, **B**, **C** and **D**. Choose the **ONE** that best completes the sentence.*

1~4   B   C   D   C   5~8   B   A   A   C

Part 3   Translation

Directions: *Translate the following sentences into English.*

1. Men couldn't fly as easily as birds because men's bodies are much heavier than them.
2. We didn't understand that question until the teacher told us the answer.
3. A jet plane usually has several engines, so it is very powerful.
4. Hydrogen is always used to fill balloons because it is cheap and light.
5. A big fire broke out because of the escape of the gas in this city last year.

Writing Practice

Directions: *Write a composition on the topic: **"The Telephone"**. You should write at least 120 words according to the suggestions given below.*

Sample

The Telephone

　The telephone is one of the most common means of communication. It is the greatest carrier of messages. Many people use it almost every day. I can hardly imagine how we would get on if we didn't have telephones.

There are some advantages of telephones. The first is speed and the second is directness. If you want to get an immediate connection, it is obviously quicker to phone someone rather than to write a letter. If you want information, it is often possible to get it directly by telephone. Another advantage is that the telephone can give you a personal feeling. If you want to speak or get in contact with a friend or a relative, you feel much closer to them when you are talking to them on the telephone, whereas in a letter, the words you write down are rather impersonal.

However, telephones have some disadvantages. If you have a telephone at home, it often rings at an inconvenient time. The telephone may ring when you are watching your favorite television program. Another disadvantage is that sometimes you might misunderstand what somebody is saying. If it is a matter of really important information, it is probably safer to have it in a letter rather than on telephone.

(209 words)

Further Practice

Part 1　Multiple Choice

Directions: *There are 10 incomplete sentences in this part. For each sentence there are four choices marked A, B, C and D. Choose the ONE that best completes the sentence.*

1~5　A　D　A　B　B　　　6~10　D　B　D　C　A

Part 2　Cloze

Directions: *There are 10 blanks in the following passage. For each blank there are four choices marked A, B, C and D. Choose the one that best fits into the passage.*

1~5　C　D　B　C　D　　　6~10　A　D　B　B　A

Part 3　Reading Comprehension

Directions: *Choose the best answer after reading the following passage.*

1~5　B　C　D　B　A

Unit 9 *Negotiation*

Key & Difficult Points：(重点、难点)

New Words

bargain, customer, concession, reasonable, quality, lack, credibility, diffuse, congratulate, commandment, prospective, likelihood, association, priority, determine, candidate, immeasurable

Phrases & Expressions

be/get used to..., preferential treatment, technological requirement, be better off doing something, take advantage of, deal with, back off, bottom line, even if, immeasurable harm, likely 的用法, as if/as though 的用法。

Exercises

Listening Practice：Section B(Exercise 1)
Reading Practice：**Text A**　Part 2　Words & Structure (Exercise)
　　　　　　　　　　　Part 3　Translation (Exercise 2)
　　　　　　　　Text B　Part 2　Words & Structure (Exercise 1, 2)
　　　　　　　　　　　Part 3　Translation (Exercise 2)
Writing Practice
Further Practice：Part 1　Multiple Choice
　　　　　　　　Part 2　Cloze

Listening Practice

Section A

Key to

Exercise

Directions: *You will hear five sentences. After you hear a sentence, read the four possible answers in your book and choose the best one to the question you have heard.*

1~5 D C B A C

Tape-script

1. I write more beautifully than George, but not as nicely as Kate.
2. Cliff does better than Joe on these tests, I think.
3. The days in the winter are shorter than in the summer.
4. The narrow balcony was more crowded with plants than people.
5. The old man eats more dinner than his wife, but less than I give him to eat.

Section B

A Will

Key to

Exercise 1

Directions: *Listen to the passage once and decide whether the following statements are true or false. Write "T" for True and "F" for False.*

1~4 T T F F

Exercise 2

Directions: *Listen to the passage again and answer the question.*

Could you tell us how to solve the problem?

The result was: The youngest got 9 horses; the second got 6 and the oldest got 2. The three brothers were all satisfied when they got exactly their own share of the horses. What they got added up to neither more nor less than 17 horses.

Tape-script

There was an old man who had three sons and seventeen horses. When he dies, the will was opened. In his will he gave the following instruction: The horses were to be divided like this—a half to his youngest son, Jack; a third to his second son John and a ninth to his eldest son Ted. The three brothers could not see how this was possible. Then they went to a wise man and asked his advice. "I will give you a horse," said the wise man, "now go away and obey your father's will."

They took the horse and went away. They now had eighteen horses and did as the will told. After that they gave the horse back.

Oral Practice

参考译文

对话 1

> **情景**
>
> 　　梁先生是一家中国公司的营销部经理,他所在的公司正在向美国市场出口产品。买方代表乔在梁先生的办公室和梁先生还价。

乔:我们是不喜欢讨价还价的,但这么高的价格我们实在无法接受。

梁:你们是我们的老顾客,如果订货的数量大,可以考虑给你特价优待。这样行了吧?

乔:这样吧,双方都做一定的让步。各让一步怎么样?

梁:呀! 若差距这么大,恐怕难以成交。

对话 2

情景

梁先生和乔再次会面。他们依旧就价格问题进行着激烈的谈判。乔正在要求更低的价格。

梁：你们认为我们产品的价格可以接受吗？

乔：你们的产品在技术方面基本符合我们的要求。但在定价方面能不能再压一压？

梁：说实在的，我给你们的价钱已经是低于市价了。请看看，这是今天报纸上的行情。

乔：我们也收到了别的供应商的报价。人家的报价就比你们便宜。

梁：相信你们不会不考虑到质量的差距吧？

Reading Practice

Text A

参考译文

如何成为精明的谈判人员

让对方先出牌

假如你能让对方先表明立场，你会处于优势地位。原因如下：

- 他们的出价也许比你预先估计的要好。
- 你可以在出牌前了解对方的情况。
- 你可以因此就他们的提议挑刺。假如他们先报价的话，你可以提出反对意见，如果双方最后就价格问题折中的话，你的目的就达到了。

大智若愚

对于聪明的谈判员来说，扮精明就是傻瓜，装傻就是精明。谈判时，你不要显得比别人能干，而要显得逊于对方，这样你就能处于优势地位。你越是糊涂，就越是对你有利，但不要弄得太过火，那样反倒会弄巧成拙，没人信。这么做是有原因的。一般情形下，人类乐于帮助那些看起来有些笨、懂得不多的人，一般不会趁机去占人便宜。大多数人都不愿与他们认为有些迟钝的人竞争，甚至还会去帮助他

203

们。因此,装傻能分散对手的竞争心理。

考虑实际的总体价位,但只说单位价格,以迷惑对手

谈论价格的方式很多。假如你向波音航空公司询问飞越太平洋的成本,公司不会明白地告诉你"52000 美元"。他们会跟你说每个乘客每英里只需花费 11 分钱。销售人员称之为价格单位化,以此来迷惑消费者。聪明的谈判员只会考虑总体价位。如果供货商只告诉你稍稍增加了一点产品的单价,你可能不会很在意这个问题。但要是你考虑到你每年购买的数量,那你就会发现这将是一大笔费用,值得你好好跟对方谈谈了。

一定要祝贺对手

谈判结束后,记住要祝贺你的对手。不管你觉得对方的表现如何糟糕,你都要祝贺他。"啊,你干得真不赖,我本可以拿出更好的交易,但老实说,这还是值得的,我毕竟从谈判中学到不少东西。你很出色。"你要让对方觉得他赢了谈判。

Exercises

Part 1　Reading Comprehension

Directions: *Read the passage once and decide whether the following statements are true or false. Write "**T**" for True and "**F**" for False.*

1~4　F　F　F　T

Part 2　Words & Structure

Directions: *Choose the correct words or phrases to complete the following sentences and change the form where necessary.*

1. split the difference　2 make concession　3. implement　4. enter into

5. commit　　　　　6. credibility　　7 fantastic

Part 3　Translation

1. Directions: *Translate the following passage into Chinese.*

事事都离不了谈判,谈判无时无地不在,其中以国际商务谈判为要。由于商业在范围和程度上越来越国际化,国际商业谈判也越来越频繁。对于许多大机构来说,国际商务谈判是司空见惯的,而不是偶尔为之的稀罕事。

2. Directions: *Translate the following sentences into English.*

1) To show our sincerity in doing business with you, we'll make an exception

this time and agree to make a further reduction of 2%. This is the best we can do.

2) If you stand firm, there's no point in further discussions. We might as well call the whole deal off.

3) I'm sorry I'm not authorized to make such a bid reduction.

4) We have received offers much lower than yours. So business depends very much on your price.

Text B

参考译文

谈判实用技巧

无论是何种经济气候下的谈判,以下的谈判戒律都能在谈判中给予你帮助,这包括:

1. 做好准备。你所掌握的市场价值和预期目标的信息越多,你的胜算就越大。你可以在互联网上、公共图书馆里收寻到大量的信息,你还可以通过不同的机构和集团网络来获取信息。花费在学习如何谈判和如何准备谈判将会是你所做的最好的投资。

2. 了解双方的需要。想要在谈判中获胜,你需要明白自己的优势,你真正想要什么? 你是否能适时掌握经济上不停地摇摆? 了解自己的需要将会帮助你决定其谈判的方式,认识并掌握你已经拥有的东西,这就能确定自己所能承受的问题。

3. 了解每个不同谈判的动态。有时你所掌握的技能是很抢手的,而有时你有可能只是对手所高兴合作或愿意交易的几个合格的候选人之一。了解了这些状况和各个对手之间相关的地位将会帮你决定如何运用自己的优势以及什么时候应该暂且后退。

4. 不置可否是你的优势。关于你方的底线你传达给对手的信息越多,你的局限性就越大。不透露出确切的现实状态,或者那些能够让步的方面,你就能逼你的对手开出最好的价来。

5. 以目标而不是赢为主。有太多的谈判更多地为了获胜而并非实现目标。记住不要让你的对手感觉到他似乎在谈判中是输家。如果你在整个过程之中疏远你以后的伙伴,你将在多方面收获其小。

6. 明白什么时候停止议价。一个肯定会让你失掉一切的东西就是贪婪。在任何谈判之中的一个基本点就是得到你应该得到的那部分即可。过分贪婪或不切实际会导致谈判的散伙，就是不散，对你也是不可估量的损害。

　　7。记住谈判是团队协作。它需要专门技能、交际能力、团队精神和在任何专业运动之中都需要的合法小把戏。

Exercises

Part 1　Reading Comprehension

Directions: *Read the passage once and decide whether the following statements are true or false. Write "T" for True and "F" for False.*

1~4　F　F　T　F

Part 2　Words & Structure

1. Directions: *Match an expression in Column B which is similar in meaning to the one in Column A.*

1)~5)　d　c　i　b　a　　　6)~10)　j　h　g　f　e

2. Directions: *Fill in each of the blanks with an appropriate word or phrase from the box. Change the form if necessary.*

1) likelihood　　　　2) dealing with　　　　3) priority

4) even if　　　　　5) determined　　　　　6) bargain

Part 3　Translation

1. Directions: *Translate the following passage into Chinese.*

　　谈判班子以外有些人可以不在谈判桌上露面，但却要参与谈判重大问题的讨论，这就是所谓"后台"角色。谈判人员要代表整个组织（或国家）的利益，有关重大问题的决定，要经常与总部联系，与"后台"人员达成一致。同时，重大谈判也要求有"后台"班子的参与，协助讨论对策，因为往往是"当局者迷，旁观者清"。"台后"人员的意见往往对"台前"人员的意见有重大影响。

2. Directions: *Translate the following sentences into English.*

1) As far as I know, the present market is rather favorable to us.

2) We'd better not make a decision and keep the choice open until we have gotten more information.

3) Please send an agenda to them and let them know our plan and sound out their opinions about it.

4) We can never be too careful. Homer sometimes nods.

5) It is high time that we shall decide who is going to involve in the negotiation.

Writing Practice

Directions: *You work for a company which is going to buy a set of equipment from China. You are asked to translate a lot of specifications and instructions within four months, which is impossible. Therefore you decide to advertise for two experienced translators as soon as possible.*

1. Write a short note to Mr. Max Remington, the Public Relation's manager. Ask for an advertisement for two translators. You should write 30~40 words.

2. Explain the reason.

3. Mention your urgency.

Sample

Dear Mr. Max Remington,

As our company is purchasing a set of equipment, a lot of materials have to be translated, which is impossible to do within four months. Could you advertise for two experienced translator in the newspapers? It is urgent.

XXX

(42 words)

Further Practice

Part 1   Multiple Choice

Directions: *There are 10 incomplete sentences in this part. For each sentence there are four choices marked **A**, **B**, **C** and **D**. Choose the **ONE** that best* *completes the sentence.*

1~5 C B D D B   6~10 B A C B C

Part 2   Cloze

Directions: *There are 10 blanks in the following passage. For each blank there are four choices marked A, B, C, and D. You should choose the **ONE** that best fits into the passage.*

  1~5 A A A D C   6~10 B A D C D
11~15 C B B C A   16~20 D C C B D

Part 3   Reading Comprehension

Directions: *Choose the best answer after reading the following passage.*

1. C 2. A 3. B 4. A 5. B 6. B 7. C

Unit 10 *Future Planning*

Key & Difficult Points：(重点、难点)

New Words

firm, break, notification, tip, employer, concise, instance, make-up, resume, website, recruit, daydream, lawyer, smart, international, realize, initially

Phrases & Expressions

apply for, keep in touch, come across, settle down, move on, run out of, familiar with, get stuck in, make one's way, follow up, dream about, turn out, choose to, have been doing 现在完成进行时的用法，"be＋不定式"结构，助动词 do 表示强调

Exercises

Listening Practice：Section A(Exercise 1,Exercise 2)
Reading Practice：**Text A**   Part 2   Words & Structure (Exercises 1,2)
                          Part 3   Translation (Exercise 2)
              Text B   Part 2   Words & Structure (Exercises 1,2)
                          Part 3   Translation (Exercise 1)
Writing Practice
Further Practice：Part 1   Multiple Choice
                  Part 2   Cloze

Listening Practice

Section A

Key to

Exercise 1

Directions: *Listen to the conversations and choose the best answer to complete each of the following statements.*

1~5　C　B　C　C　C

Tape-script

1. W: Your brother graduated in 1996. What about you?
   M: I finished school a year later.
2. M: What happened to Terry? He's sad.
   W: He didn't get accepted by any of the colleges he really wanted to go to.
3. W: Which subject do you like best, Henry?
   M: I prefer music to math and physics.
4. M: Didn't you go to class tonight?
   W: When I arrived, the class had already finished.
5. M: I always get nervous when I take a test.
   M: Don't worry. You always do well in English.

Exercise 2

Directions: *Listen to a dialogue and choose the best answer to each of the following questions.*

1~3　C　B　C

Tape-script

W: What do you do, Tom?
M: I'm a secretary.
W: Did you go to a university?
M: Oh, yes. I went to a university for four years. Dad wanted me to become a

doctor but I didn't like the idea.

W: What happened?

M: I didn't think I could get enough money to study for five years.

W: Have you worked for the same company since you finished your university?

M: Yes, I have. Why don't we talk about you now?

Section B

Key to

Exercise

Directions: *Complete the following dialogue according to what you hear.*

(1) puzzled   (2) think   (3) about   (4) other

(5) things   (6) clock   (7) on   (8) the

(9) wall   (10) plan   (11) things   (12) well

Tape-script

John: My boss told me not to go to work again.

Lucy: I can't believe it. Why?

John: I don't know. When he told me that, I was so puzzled.

Lucy: Did you usually go to work late?

John: Well, I often did.

Lucy: When you did your work, did you think about other things?

John: Sometimes.

Lucy: How often did you look at the clock on the wall?

John: Every ten minutes.

Lucy: Could you use a computer?

John: No. I can only use a typewriter.

Lucy: Well, I think I know why now. You didn't use your time well and didn't plan things well.

John: Really?

Lucy: I'm sure.

Oral Practice

参考译文

对话1

> **情景**
>
> 约翰·史密斯是美国人。他正为一份到中国工作的职业和经理面谈。

经理：你应聘哪个部门？

约翰：我是应聘市场调查的。

经理：你有这方面的工作经验吗？

约翰：在美国时，我在市场调查公司呆了三年。

经理：你以前在中国工作过吗？你会讲中文吗？

约翰：没有。日常的会话没问题。

经理：我来说一下工作条件。上班时间是早上9点到下午5点。

约翰：休息时间有多久？

经理：中午有1小时的午餐时间，3点钟有15分钟的休息。

约翰：每周工作5天吗？

经理：是，从第二年起，你就有带薪假期。

约翰：那很公平。

经理：如果你被录用，后天可以接到通知书。

对话2

> **情景**
>
> 汤姆和简是同事。汤姆正在和简谈论他的老朋友。

汤姆：我在找一些老朋友的下落。

简：　你没有和他们保持联络吗？

汤姆：没有，我们失去了联络。

简： 你没有遇见他们任何一个吗？

汤姆：见过几次。他们有的过得很稳定，有的被生活、工作牵制，有的尽情享受人生，有的过着一成不变的生活。

简： 希望有一天你可以和他们把酒言欢。

Reading Practice

Text A

参考译文

在人才招聘会上获得成功的技巧

在人才招聘会上所犯的错误可能会使最好的应聘者落选，得不到她或他想要的工作、下面 10 条技巧也许能帮助你在招聘会上获得成功。

1. 做商业广告。你有 30 秒的时间让某位雇主对你感兴趣。如果你做不到，他们会另寻他人。准备一个 30 秒钟的广告介绍你自己和你的事业目标。简洁明了，但要有具体的例子抓住对方的注意力。

2. 看上去具有职业形象。不要化妆太浓。一旦你清楚了某公司的文化后，你才可以决定是否化妆。

3. 带上至少 50 份个人简历。首页介绍在招聘会上并非必备，但也不能冒缺少简历的危险。

4. 带上一个书包，一本笔记本和一支笔。书包用来装文献和赠品。笔记本应该是办公用的，有足够的地方妥善保管你的个人简历（请不要把简历弄得皱巴巴的），还有一个便签簿。带两支笔以备万一。

5. 休息好。头天晚上充分休息，以便精力充沛地参加人才招聘会。

6. 做好应聘准备。上网查找参加招聘会的公司的资料，以便熟悉他们，知道他们在招聘什么样的雇员。

7. 提前到达。人才招聘会往往会吸引数以千计、万计的人前往。争取早到，抢一份目录单，计划你的主攻目标。

8. "反其道而行之"。许多人陷入前门拥挤慌乱的人群中难以脱身。你不妨直接走向后门，那里有代表们等候来访者的出现。

9. 拿宣传品和商务名片。只拿那些你感兴趣的公司的宣传品，因为你会阅读他们。不要忘记拿商务名片，因为日后你可以和招聘人联系。

10. 表达你的兴趣。握手要有力,直视对方微笑。这是极好的第一印象,且能表现你的自信心。要问问题。没有什么比一方侃侃而谈,一方沉默无语更没意思的了。主动做后续工作,不要等公司给你打电话——先打给他们,商定面试或参观公司等事宜。

Exercises

Part 1　Reading Comprehension

Directions: *Decide whether the following statements are true or false according to the text. Write "**T**" for True and "**F**" for False.*

1~5　T　F　T　T　T

Part 2　Words and Structure

1. Directions: *Match an expression in* **Column B** *which is similar in meaning to the one in* **Column A**.

1)~5)　c　a　b　g　d　　　　6)~10)　e　j　i　h　f

2. Directions: *Fill in each of the blanks with an appropriate word or phrase from the box. Change the form if necessary.*

1) commercial 　　　　　　2) moved on

3) follow up 　　　　　　　4) employees

5) make my way 　　　　　6) picked up

7) professional 　　　　　　8) make-up

9) risk 　　　　　　　　　10) recruiting

Part 3　Translation

1. Directions: *Translate the following sentences into Chinese.*

1) 你有 30 秒的时间让某位雇主对你感兴趣。如果你不能做到,他们会另寻他人。

2) 头天晚上充分休息,以便精力充沛地参加人才招聘会。

3) 上网查找参加招聘会的公司的资料,以便熟悉他们,知道他们在招聘什么样的雇员。

4) 不要忘记拿商务名片,因为日后你可以和招聘人联系。

5) 主动做后续工作,不要等公司给你打电话——先打给他们。

2. Directions: *Translate the following sentences into English.*

1) We are looking for an improvement in your work this term.

2) We are running out of petrol.

3) I'll wait for you in the garden this afternoon.

4) It may rain — you'd better take an umbrella in case.

5) I'm not very familiar with these terms.

Text B

参考译文

对生活的期望

想过 10 年以后你会在哪里吗？15 年 20 年后呢？确切地知道你将会在哪里，你将要做什么是很困难的，但是每个人都会幻想未来，你可能在将要毕业的时候想象未来的工作；你可能梦想着遇见你的人生伴侣或者是居住在一个海边的大房子里。

十几岁时，我和我的朋友都在展望 2000 年。新世纪到来时，我们会很快成为 40 多岁的人，这似乎有些老了。我曾经告诉我的朋友我将成为一个富有的律师，并且有一对双胞胎——一个男孩和一个女孩，每个人都会对我和我美丽的妻子称赞我们的孩子是多么聪明。

在我的梦里，我们住在一个两层的大房子里，地板和楼梯都是木制的。我想象每一年我们都可以拥有最高的圣诞树。我的理想居室里有一个宽敞的客厅——家人和朋友们可以随时来拜访我。现在，46 岁的我回首过去的梦想笑了。因为我梦想的东西都没有完全实现，但是我不会为了梦想中的世界而改变我现在所拥有的。

大学里，我学习的是国际贸易并且计划考取法律院校。在我大学三年级那年，我意识到我并不想成为一名律师，而是想成为一名语言教师。语言教得越多，我越觉得我想成为教授语言教师的教师。现在，我是一名大学教授，负责培训那些将英语作为外语教授的老师。

我结婚了，有了不止两个孩子。我和我的妻子最初讨论拥有一个 8 个到 10 个孩子的大家庭。最后，我们有了 5 个孩子。我是否住在有木质地板的梦想房子里？不，我不是，但是我爱我的家并且不希望搬到其他任何地方去住。

我认为，作为一个年轻人，拥有理想并且为之制定相应的计划是很重要的。然而，能够意识到并不是所有的梦想都会像你设想的那样实现同样重要。我生命里学到的重要的一课是:为你所拥有的感到快乐。

Exercises

Part 1　Reading Comprehension

Directions: *Decide whether the following statements are true or false according to the text. Write "**T**" for True and "**F**" for False.*

1~5　T　F　F　T　T

Part 2　Words and Structure

1. Directions: *Match an expression in **Column B** which is similar in meaning to the one in **Column A**.*

1~5　b　d　a　e　c

2. Directions: *Fill in each of the blanks with an appropriate word or phrase from the box. Change the form if necessary.*

1) professor　　　　　　2) turns out

3) lawyer　　　　　　　4) daydream

5) chose to

Part 3　Translation

1. Directions: *Translate the following paragraph into Chinese.*

　　我认为,作为一个年轻人,拥有理想并且为之制定相应的计划是很重要的。然而,能够意识到并不是所有的梦想都会像你设想的那样实现同样重要。我生命里学到了重要的一课是:为你所拥有的感到快乐。

2. Directions: *Translate the following sentences into English.*

1) What did you dream about last night?

2) We're so much looking forward to seeing you again.

3) She's planning to visit her sister in England next year.

4) The boy has been trained for five years.

5) She came initially to spend a few days, but in the end she stayed for a whole month.

Writing Practice

Directions: *Write an application letter according to your own personal information. You should write no less than 100 words.*

Sample

March 25, 2005

Manager of Human Resources

The Youth Travel Agency

Beijing, 100060

Dear Sir or Madam:

I'm writing to apply for the secretary position mentioned in your advertisement in China Daily (March 20th).

I shall graduate from the college, finishing the requirements in three years, during which I have equipped myself with a profound knowledge of tourism service and management. My studies have included courses in tourism psychology, tourism laws and regulations and so forth.

Though I have no business experience, I believe that I have the training and qualities that you are looking for. I am good at computer operating and have a knowledge of tourism management.

I shall be glad to call at any time for an interview.

Very truly yours,

Li Li

(126 words)

求职信的要素：

1. 介绍消息来源

介绍消息来源实际上是求职信的开篇交待句，它可使求职信显得自然、顺畅；而不介绍消息来源，会使收信人感到意外、突然，文章也缺乏过渡、照应。如：

Dear manager,

I learned from the newspaper that your company wanted to hire an English translator.

2. 表明求职心愿

介绍完消息来源后，应向收信人表明自己的求职心愿，即写信的目的。

3. 介绍个人简历

4. 摆出求职优势

　　求职时应表明自己的优势和特长，及是否有工作经历等。

5. 提出获职打算

　　丰富的工作经验，一定的优势和特长，只能代表过去和现在，如果获职后高枕无忧，马虎从事，也得不到用人单位的认可。表明获职后努力工作的决心是谋得工作的重要一环。

6. 请求答复联系

7. 表明感激之情

　　无论请求是否能够得到满意的答复，给用人单位写信就是给对方添了麻烦，因此应向对方表明感激之情。

Further Practice

Part 1　Multiple Choice

Directions: *There are 10 incomplete sentences in this part. For each sentence there are four choices marked **A**, **B**, **C** and **D**. Choose the **ONE** that best completes the sentence.*

1~5　A　A　C　D　B　　　　6~10　C　B　C　B　D

Part 2　Cloze

Directions: *There are 20 blanks in the following passage. For each blank there are four choices marked **A**, **B**, **C**, and **D**. You should choose the **ONE** that best fits into the passage.*

　1~5　B　C　C　A　B　　　　6~10　D　D　A　C　B

11~15　C　D　D　C　A　　　　16~20　C　B　D　C　A

Part 3　Reading Comprehension

Directions: *Choose the best answer after reading the following passage.*

1~5　C　B　C　B　C